Walter Lübeck

The Tao of Money

The Spiritual Approach to Money, Occupation, and Possessions
as a Means of Personal and Social Transformation

Translated by Christine M. Grimm

LOTUS PRESS
SHANGRI-LA

The Author – Walter Lübeck

Walter Lübeck has been active as a seminar leader for alternative methods of healing, holistic personality development, and success training since 1988. Since then, more than 8000 participants have attended his seminars, lectures, and workshops in Germany, Austria, Switzerland, Hungary, and the Netherlands.

The results of Walter Lübeck's work have been made available to the broad public in his 19 books, which have been translated into 13 languages, and numerous articles in specialized magazines. His professional background includes training as a naturopath, 10 years of studying classical and complex homeopathy, as well as phytotherapy, NLP training, and more than 15 years of involvement with Reiki, alternative therapies and healthy nutrition.

First English Edition 2000
© by Lotus Press, Box 325, Twin Lakes, WI 53181, USA
The Shangri-La Series is published in cooperation
with Schneelöwe Verlagsberatung, Federal Republic of Germany
©1992 by Windpferd Verlagsgesellschaft mbH, Aitrang, Germany
All rights reserved
Translated by Christine M. Grimm
Cover design by Kuhn Grafik, Zürich
Interior illustrations: Roland Tietsch

ISBN 0-914955-62-4
Library of Congress Catalog Number 99-97282

Printed in USA

Table of Contents

INTRODUCTION

The TAO of the Dollar—Spiritual Development Through a Loving and Conscious Approach to Money

Dealing with money has always been vitally important to my progress on the spiritual path. This process has taught me how to love. It lets God work within me and through me. By confronting the themes of money, occupation, and possessions, I have also learned a great deal about esotericism. This gives me a better, more complete understanding of the world. According to the ancient spiritual law of Hermes Trismegistus "as within, so without," I have learned to observe people's behavior toward money and possessions: They directly express their personal attitudes toward fear, responsibility, and love in how they treat their material goods.

Do we basically respect our own achievements and the achievements of others as a contribution to growth in the world? Do we give and take money, which represents this achievement, with the desire of using it to consciously spread loving and creative energy within ourselves and among our fellow human beings? Or are we mainly concerned with filling up our bank account? Do we hoard possessions without using them to create the opportunities for growth in harmony for others and ourselves? Do we discover and express talents, thereby contributing to the advancement of peace and freedom? Or do we even care whether there is an equally valuable return service for the money that we receive? Do we deceive others and ourselves through our fear of getting a bad deal?

The right approach to money and everything related to it—which I believe to be the spiritual approach—can become the most powerful and beautiful exercise for developing our personality.

We will become bringers of light if we understand the hidden, esoteric meaning found in the flow of money—and if we turn giving and taking into an energy exercise. We will impart positive vibrations to everyone with whom we come in contact. We can recognize and use the money path, the TAO of money, for ourselves. This path can help us recognize the ubiquitous medium of money as a bringer of blessings.

Money is minted freedom. (Dostoevsky)

This sentence is always valid when we charge money with love and spread positive energy with it. Nothing that human beings have created is distributed as extensively, and has been so ignorantly misused, as money. Now, on the threshold of the Age of Aquarius, we can finally learn to use this wonderful opportunity to heal the environment and the society in which we live. We can use it to heal ourselves, becoming attuned to a higher level of vibrations. Many people would like to make a contribution to world peace, but cannot find an effective way or have found one that has only been marginally effective up to now. So here is a new approach! This is a path that many people are aware of but frequently misunderstand and reject. Yet, it is a path that still has all of its opportunities waiting for us. Almost every one of us comes into contact with money on a daily basis. We are exposed to the energy patterns transported by this medium, and these patterns exert their influence on us.

Money is a form of energy storage. (Culkin)

Money is basically neutral, it only acquires a certain quality through the way in which we use it. According to whether we spend it with love, consciousness, and responsibility as we participate in its flow or thoughtlessly squander it, it spreads light or darkness. In order to use this opportunity, we don't need to have a great deal of money: We can take this approach even if we don't have much of it—and particularly if we are in this situation or have problems with it. We will quickly sense how money that is spent and accepted with love radiates energy much better than money charged with a lack of awareness. Time and again, this approach will charm a smile onto other people's faces. It allows us to feel interpersonal warmth when we deal with light-charged money. Yet, this isn't the only thing! Since the loving way in which we deal with money and possessions makes us more and more friends and allies, our financial worries will melt away like snow in the sun!

7

The more people there are who live the law of love, the law of God in our lives, the more happiness-creating abundance there will be in the world.

My Personal Money Path

Before we explore the path of money in the following chapters, I'd like to tell you about my own personal money path.

My conscious money path began one beautiful summer day when I was six years old. My father asked me to help him build a covered bird table for the birds in our garden. After the work was completed, he put a dollar in my little hand with the words: "You did that well and you should get something for it!" I happily ran to the store with my "treasure" and bought myself an ice cream with it. The shopkeeper asked me who gave me the money. When I responded that my father had paid me for my work, the man smiled and shared in my happiness. Although this experience may sound rather banal to many people, I had received a much greater fortune than the dollar, namely a feeling of self-worth, which no one could ever take away from me again.

Years later, when I was a teenager and attended high school, I learned how to supplement the very limited amount of pocket money I received (because of a financial emergency in my family at that time): I tutored others in various subjects. While helping younger students get better grades, I had fun studying with them because I saw no reason why learning shouldn't be enjoyable. In addition to money they paid me, satisfied parents repeatedly gave me little presents as recognition of this accomplishment. These experiences had quite an impact on me. Through activities that were meaningful and brought me joy, I developed a positive attitude toward self-reliance and personal financial responsibility.

Since that time, my first question always is how I can earn the means that I require to fulfill my needs instead of complaining that others don't take care of me. This attitude has given me independence, freedom, and much satisfaction in my life. I have frequently experienced "coincidences" that help me when I assume responsibility for my personal economic situation by making holistically valuable contributions.

When I was about 15 years old, I began to invest in stocks. At first, I did this together with my older brother; later I tried it on my own. For a time, I was very successful, perhaps because of the proverbial beginner's luck. But this may also have been because my inner child was so fascinated by such a great game: It often gave me important information through its extrasensory capabilities. In my youthful naiveté, I was quickly seized by the intoxication of "fast money." In my search for profitable investment objects, I devoured the pertinent securities newspapers every morning before school at the railway station newsstand. However, the greedier I became in the process, the more my luck deserted me. Since I naturally didn't understand the psychological and spiritual correlations at that time, I looked for the reason in my lack of technical comprehension. But in my fixation on profits, I had completely overlooked the fact that the ventures at the beginning of my "stock-market career," when I practically had no idea about financial investments, had been much more successful than later, when I crammed myself with expertise and up-to-date information. I read numerous books about the stock market and economics. In addition, I was a young participant at many regional and international seminars about financial investments. I wanted to finally find the philosopher's stone of the stock market and "cash in" on business in a big way. In my mind, I saw myself with a Davidoff cigar (which would certainly have made me sick), sitting in a Porsche (which I wouldn't have been allowed to drive because of my age), and playing the part of the playboy (which I now know would have had an impoverishing effect on my life and ultimately led me astray in a rather unpleasant way).

An unconscious approach to our needs makes us a slave of money!

Does this unrealistic, starry-eyed dreamer approach sound familiar to you? It's no wonder since many people often wish for countless things that are neither good for them nor truly useful. However, if you examine what actually interests them, you will discover that completely different, simpler and more human wishes are behind the goals for which they superficially strive. Most people are firmly convinced that they will receive affection, eroticism, love, security, and recognition along with the spacious house, the stylish car, the expensive hi-fi system, and the fashionable clothing. This ersatz game

9

is also put to systematic use by advertising. Just take a close and conscious look at how products are sold.

Before I went on to study economics, I joined the sales organization of a large insurance company. Here I gathered about two intensive years of experiences with people and their relationships to money, prestige, and security. These two years were quite important for my later development. In this line of business, dynamic people with a certain character structure and a little luck can very quickly earn quite a lot of money. Consequently, it was possible for me to do wonderful studies on myself and others about greed, envy, fear, image neurosis, addiction to power, and the resulting hierarchical structures with their related human problems.

Then, during my time at the university, I learned to recognize these energies on a greater scale, namely in terms of national economy and business management. During these years, I was still driven by my greed for money and possessions to be involved in economic matters. Since I was also primarily concerned with "making money," I broke off my studies after five semesters. I had noticed that the theoretical wisdom of the university couldn't be turned into hard cash since it was too difficult to put it into direct practice.

As a result, I became self-employed together with two older partners in the area of oil-field and mining equipment. Yet, I had still learned during my "academic years" that theories, even if they come from the most famous of people, are not necessarily important or right for everyday use. (This perception also helped me repeatedly in separating the wheat from the chaff when I became involved with metaphysics.) For more than six years, I was quite successful at our company in the areas of sales, advertising, and product design. The business grew and grew. But despite this, an increasingly strong feeling of unease spread within me over the course of time. At first it was still quite indistinct and weak. But then body and soul, in an increasingly concrete and intense manner, rebelled against my way of dealing with work, occupation, and money. Moreover, I developed difficulties in my private life and a severe metabolic disorder. I suffered on all levels of my being, to the point where I verged on giving myself up for lost. Because of my misery, I had to find new ways of approaching my life.

Wealth is not found in the possession of treasures, but in the way we know how to use them. (Napoleon I)

Within two years of strenuous work on myself, I was able to better integrate spirituality (which I had limited to a few narrowly defined areas of life) into my everyday life. Somehow, the enormous pressure of suffering had untied the knot of my unconscious state. I now finally understood that I had to translate love, personal responsibility, and freedom—meaning God – into reality in my life if I didn't want to vegetate as an unhappy and bitter person. I wanted to find the place in life that was appropriate for me. Consequently, with the help of my spiritual teacher and an intensive physically oriented psychotherapy, I prepared for the fundamental professional and private restructuring of my life. Consequently, this occurred with almost no problems. During this time, I also received initiations into the first two Reiki degrees.*

Afterward, I experienced a real leap in development. Ways of behaving that I simply hadn't been able to harmonize before now practically changed overnight, giving me unbelievable new opportunities for living in a free and more loving manner. Strengthened in this way, I started my first esoteric profession: I became the publisher of a regional esoteric magazine.

As a result of this new occupation, I came into intensive contact with the esoteric scene. Sensitized by my previous experiences, I rather quickly noticed the problems that many people involved in the New Age scene had with money, occupation, and possessions. Apparently, an interest in spirituality—or even a spiritually oriented occupation—doesn't mean that a person can also treat material things in a loving and conscious manner. To the contrary, I often had the impression that particularly in the esoteric scene, there were substantial problems in this respect. Some people thought that money, interest, and possessions were the roots of all evil in the world and wanted to abolish them. Unfortunately, in the process they overlooked that the way in which people use material goods make them into bringers of blessings or disaster. (More on this in the next chapter.)

---

* Reiki is an old Asiatic method of conveying universal life energy for the purposes of healing and personality development. Also see my books: "Reiki—Way of the Heart" and "The Complete Reiki Handbook" published by Lotus Light/Shangri-La.

Some time later, I began training for the 3rd Reiki Degree (Master/Teacher), completing it after one year with the respective initiation. My emotions during the first seminars that I was now permitted to give confirmed a feeling that I had already had for a long time: This was my place in the world. This was where I was content and could spread happiness! My life as a publisher soon came to an end after this time, and I became completely involved in my profession as a Reiki Master and author.

Not what a person acquires with his work is the actual reward of a human being, but what he becomes as a result of it. (Ruskin)

Today, some years later, I am still very glad that I have taken this path. Things have never been so good for me. I am allowed to do what fills my heart with joy, and I can live well from it. Many interesting things have happened to me, allowing me to experience the flow of life as a wonderfully exciting adventure.

As you can see, even though it wasn't necessarily oriented directly toward a previously defined goal, my path had many twists and turns to it. Among other things, it was quite strenuous, especially when I hadn't yet consciously opened myself to practicing spirituality in my everyday life. But this dynamic force in my experiences gave me the possibility of untying the knots of my unconscious state. It gave me a better comprehension of life's true laws, and I've learned to accept my place here in the world. These perceptions help me today in holding my seminars, doing personal counseling, and writing books. It basically isn't all that difficult to be happy in the material world! I hope my experiences can help you continue developing your very own personal type of happiness.

The methods described in the following chapters work. They come from the practice and not from theoretical observations. Become familiar with them—they can help you find fulfillment in the correct approach to material goods, happiness and success, love and freedom, and ultimately God within you and your life.

Money is love in action. (Esoteric saying)

Sincerely,

Walter Fulues

Chapter 1

THE SPIRITUAL APPROACH
TO MONEY

What is Money in the Esoteric Sense?

You surely know what *money* is. After all, it has accompanied you throughout your life and you use it almost every day. Or do you let it use you? Whatever the situation may be—how can I tell you something new about money? Okay, I've earned quite a bit of it in my short life and spent a lot of it in one way or another. Would you perhaps like to have a few tips on how to get rich quick from my "experience as a millionaire"? Well, sorry, I have to disappoint you in this respect. I don't want to make you miserable by telling the lie that the more money you have, the happier you will be. In this regard, I have only achieved happiness since understanding how important it is for me to handle my "dough" in a meaningful way and not have too much or too little of it.

I would like to show you how you can treat money in order to become happy and spread happiness. To do this, you must learn to see this wonderful tool for personal and social healing in a new light. Only when we understand the spiritual dimension of money can it become a good-luck charm for us in the truest sense of the word. So what is the esoteric meaning of the dollar?

"Esoteric" is translated to mean "concealed." Important perceptions are best concealed when they are hidden in what seems to be obvious. Consequently, the esoteric meaning of money lies in its quality as a means of transporting energy, something clearly visible to everyone. Just like the blood in your body brings nutrients to each individual cell, money transports energy to the individual cells of the society effectively. It even brings it to you and me, for example. When you work and are paid for it, you receive your condensed work energy (the increased value that you have created). In turn, we can give it to others as an exchange for the variety of services that they may offer. It isn't easy to put the energy directly in your pocket, so there is a generally recognized symbol for a market value of services that corresponds to an amount of money. So what's so esoteric about it? Well, if money is a means of storing and transporting energy, and if it is charged by the personal achievement of the person who spends it, it also carries other energy qualities in addition to the "value vibration". These qualities are released by the individual way of approaching the work or the goods.*

If we throw money away on things that we actually don't need, which may even possibly harm us and others, and we aren't even clear about our actions, the money will also be charged with this vibration and influence people who come in contact with it. This influence will be more or less intensive according to the other person's strength of character, momentary state of mind, and the amount of money involved. On the other hand, joyfully and respectfully spending money in a conscious and fair way for the exchanged service, as well as satisfying the true needs of the people involved, will spread this conscious, loving, and harmonious vibration throughout society. So every time we spend money, we have the opportunity of moving our entire society a bit more in the direction of joy, consciousness, and love. Sounds great, doesn't it? And this is exactly why there is money—it is one of many wonderful opportunities for development that the Creator has put right in front of our noses, or in our hands. We only have to let go of the prejudices that have developed and understand how the harmonious, spiritual approach to money functions—and then live accordingly. In order for us to use all the opportunities that this wonderful means of personal and

---

*Esotericism has long recognized that objects are imprinted by the personal energy patterns of people who touch them. For example, on the basis of clothing that has been worn, a pendulum can be used to make apt statements about the wearer. Another example is that some people wrap their Tarot decks in insulating silk as protection against other people's energies and do not give them to anyone else without this protection. In the healing work with gemstones, they are usually cleansed energetically before use so that they only transmit the desired vibrations. Some people prefer to do spiritual exercises in a room that has been energetically balanced, if at all possible. For example, smudging with herbs (sage) or the applications of Second Degree Reiki are used for this purpose. This important knowledge can also be applied to money, which goes through so many hands and is practically saturated with many different energies.

14

social transformation offers, here are more thoughts about money from the spiritual perspective.

Why Do People Use Money?

In so-called primitive societies, there is no money; an exchange of natural products primarily occurs. Relatively few people are involved in the exchange process. The processing of the products doesn't go through very many steps and the amount of goods is relatively limited. The people involved usually know each other and are informed about the "chicken/cabbage course," for example. Directly exchanging one good for another functions within this context. The more individuals involved in this economic process, the farther away the buyer lives from the seller and the greater the variety of the goods and services, the more difficult the exchange of natural products becomes. For example, what would you think of receiving one goat, twenty eggs, two heads of cabbage, and fifteen pounds of potatoes from your employer for your work? Where would you keep all of it until you needed it? How would you use it to save for a house or a vacation? What would you do if you only needed something of little value to trade for a candle, for example—and all you had left was the goat, which the candle-seller had no use for because of his overfilled goat shed?

As we can see, in a complex society like ours it wouldn't be possible to get rid of money. Nothing would function anymore! This is exactly why clever people invented money in order to make life easier for all of us. Basically, money is energy. Wherever energy flows easily and naturally, there will hardly be any of the congestion that brings imbalances with it. Flowing water cleanses itself. Only the pond without an inlet and outlet has foul water that we can't drink without becoming ill. Many things were only made possible through the invention of money—how should, for example, donations be collected in America for the purpose of building homes in India if something like money didn't exist? If "natural products" were collected, just the cost of transporting them would be astronomical and make the sense of the entire action questionable. So abolishing money is not the answer.

Here is a summary of the advantages money offers:

- A simple exchange of goods and services
- An uncomplicated means of accumulating or saving values for larger plans
- A simple transmission of assets over large distances or greater periods of time
- An exchange value that is easily ascertainable, understandable, and relatively stable for everyone (a traded goat can die of an illness the next day, causing the value to be almost "0." On the other hand, the value of money is generally much more stable)
- Minimal space requirement

Money and Interest from the Holistic Perspective

In recent years, some radical theorists have claimed that we must abolish interest since it is the root of exploitation, social imbalances, and so forth. But we can also develop a holistic, spiritually oriented perspective on this topic. Take a look at these ideas* on "money and interest" and seriously consider them—even if you have another opinion about it, and particularly if you do. Perhaps you may find this new way of looking at things to be quite useful.

Interest as an Incentive for the Effective Use of Money

I don't want to go into the many economic reasons for interest here. There are enough good books available on the fundamental economic issues. Instead, I want to explain interest from the spiritual perspective in this section. This perspective can help us develop an entirely new, more holistic way of dealing with debts. The more people understand what really is behind loans and interest, the more quickly our economy will become an engine for spiritual development. Let's take a look at how this functions.

---

* *These naturally aren't my own ideas. I don't know more than anyone else does – I'm just applying the ancient wisdom of the great spiritual traditions to the topic of "money."*

If we need more money (energy) than we already have available to us in order for our concepts to take form, we can borrow some from a person who trusts us in return for interest. Then we are in the fortunate position of doing more than our own means would permit us to do. As a result, you are using a type of leverage. If our own financial strength is inadequate for a plan, we can do something to let the necessary energy for our plan to be implemented flow to us from our fellow human beings. In this way, the forces that other people do not need at this time can be used in order for the Creation to progress, for concepts to be turned into action and new opportunities for experience to be created.

Without this method of accessing reserves that are fallow, we would miss out on many important developmental possibilities and never have as many experiences. So lending money (energy) is an entirely sensible system. However, why should people make their collected energies available for someone else's plan without receiving a service in return? After all, they could also use this energy for themselves to increase their means and promote their own growth. A solution for this would be if someone who wants to borrow financial strength offers to let the owners receive as much energy as they believe could have been earned had they used the means themselves within the respective period of time. So this reflux of energy is called "interest!" With the means of interest, no one loses anything. In addition, through the constant drain of energy, the debtor is encouraged to handle the borrowed financial strength as effectively as possible and achieve more than the creditors would have been able to.

There is another important benefit of loans and interest. The forces of yin and yang, rest and activity, must be balanced in order for harmony to rule. In addition, these two qualities alternate on a regular basis—a time of rest is followed by a phase of activity, which is again followed by a time of rest, and so forth. The more strongly pronounced one phase is, the more intense, but in the contrasting quality, the following phase will also be. If we work with the means available to us during a yang period, we actively participate in the general process of growth and the perfection of the Creation. When we rest afterward, this is completely correct and important for us.

However, during this period of rest, our powers are largely fallow. They are not being used, and this isn't in the sense of the creative force. It always strives for applying all means in the most effective way possible in order to achieve the greatest progress in general growth and increase its quality. In addition, there will always be many people who are in their yang period at the moment. This means they are in their work phase, and perhaps could use our reserves in order to advance themselves and the rest of the world. If we make our means available to these people until we need them again ourselves, they can achieve more with their time. As a result, we leave the yin period strengthened by the interest we have collected. Equipped with greater means, we can now set more things into motion. Unless, and this is another perspective, we now have more reserves than we can meaningfully employ with our abilities. Should the surplus portion lie around uselessly because of this? Why not lease it to others for a return service and thereby increase our benefit—and that of the others—by optimally applying the available means?

This sounds pretty good, doesn't it? But couldn't we also do this without interest? Of course, all of this could function without interest, but then the human freedom of thought and action would have to be replaced by a central control system that distributes the energies in the right way. This would make us all puppets dancing according to the tune of a cosmic Secretary of Commerce. Another alternative would be perfection. If all of us and the rest of the Creation were perfect, we would need neither money nor interest, nor even this level of the Creation, the material world. I don't like either alternative, apart from the fact that neither you nor I, nor anyone else could create either of the two possibilities. I enjoy my freedom and want to have the right to make my own mistakes and learn from them. Then I can be happy about my self-made success. I would also instigate a rebellion against this kind of dictatorship since it wouldn't be very supportive of personal development.

And I don't want to be perfect either. My imperfection is precisely what gives me the opportunity to develop love, sympathy, and responsibility. I wouldn't want to miss out on that. How would you feel if you had to choose between these three paths?

Summary

• Interest helps us use the available powers as effectively as possible.
• Interest is a fair exchange for the temporary employment of other people's financial strengths, for which their own energy is not available at this time.
• Interest intensifies the awareness of our own opportunities and of acting in a responsible manner.

Money and the Root Chakra

In the system of chakras, the distribution areas for the various aspects of life energy in the body, money can largely be assigned to the root chakra. Among other things, this energy center also controls the blood in the organism. Money in the organism of the society assumes many tasks similar to those of blood in the human body, and therefore also belongs to this center. Both distribute life-promoting energies. In the widest sense, the root chakra secures survival and differentiates the functions of fighting and fleeing, species-preserving sexuality*, and solid grounding in the material world. Money can be used to secure our own survival and that of others. It creates a connection between materials since it stores energy and can be charged by constructively dealing with the various parts of the Creation (productivity).

So what can understanding the energetic classification of money do for us? For one thing, now we know where we can start if someone has chronic difficulties in dealing with money. Today we have many kinds of opportunities for harmonizing and strengthening the chakras. (If you are not familiar with this field, you can get an overview by reading one of the books mentioned in the Commented Bibliography of the Appendix.) Moreover, we can become extensively informed about the tasks of the root chakra. In the process, we can work on our level of consciousness to prevent new disorders and make it easier to heal the old ones.

As an economic correlation: the profit, the augmentation, and the improvement of material opportunities.

As long as we believe that our financial problems basically have nothing to do with the development of our personality, significant opportunities for growth remain unused. We can't really progress since we are letting our roots atrophy. In addition, when we are armed with this knowledge we can more easily experience the esoteric dimension in everyday life. In turn, this is indispensably necessary for living our spirituality.

Money work is light-energy work!

To conclude this chapter, here are a few more thoughts about applying the knowledge presented here: Theory and practice are two completely different things. Perhaps you may believe that these ideas are rather nice, but not quite applicable in practice. I have found that the more I trust myself to use the principles conveyed by spiritual teachers, the better things work out for me. I naturally had to first start out experiencing all of this on a small scale. Over time, it has extended to larger areas. Whenever I make the effort to swim along in the stream of life to the best of my ability and knowledge and contribute to the spiritualization of the world, I am rewarded with success. Just try it out for yourself! Start out with small steps and then, when you see that they work, try the larger ones. I wish you the courage and strength to take this path – both for your sake and in the interest of the rest of Creation, which urgently needs another bringer of light.

Three Key Principles for the Holistic Use of Money and Interest

1. The law of fair trade

Every service must meet with an appropriate return service to guarantee the even, harmonious distribution of energy in the universe. If the return service isn't given in a conscious and voluntary manner, disharmonies and imbalances will occur that urge for resolution to take place (development of karmic bonds!).

2. The law of wealth through love and consciousness

The more consciously and lovingly we exchange service and return service, the higher and more lasting our profit will be. The less consciously and lovingly we participate in the exchange process, the smaller our profit will be in the holistic sense.

3. The law of optimally using the cosmic forces

The unused forces of the universe can be attracted by individual beings and used to increase their personal possibilities of creation. In order for this energy re-distribution to not create any disharmonies in the stream of life, those who have benefited from it must guarantee the return of these forces to their point of origin as soon as the beneficiaries no longer need them for the realization of plans. In addition, they must let as much new energy flow back to the owners as these owners could have created with the borrowed means in the period of time that they were put to use.

Chapter 2

THE SPIRITUAL MEANING
OF WEALTH

What is Wealth in the Esoteric Sense?

There are people who think that wealth only relates to the greatest possible accumulation of money and possessions. I know people who, evaluated according to this criterion, are *very* rich. But if we understand wealth in a holistic sense, they are often bitterly impoverished.

> *The rich would be very happy if they were just half as happy as the poor believe that they are! (Charles Tschopp)*

From the spiritual perspective, people are rich who have enough material opportunities to learn everything important for them on their path; at the same time they are able to fulfill themselves by developing all of their abilities to the greatest extent. The surplus created by personal achievement and the grace of the Creator should provide the means for us to continue to grow and have our needs satisfied. This should be given to those who need more than they personally have currently available in reserve.

If we have too few material opportunities, we will miss out on important learning steps or these steps will be delayed. In addition, we won't live in a state of need and are able to give other beings the opportunities for self-fulfillment at certain times without having to do renounce the means for our own development. If we have a great deal more than we need for our experiences at the moment, we will become heavy and inflexible, like people who have too much body mass without a direct function, overweight, and drag it around with them. As a result, they can't attend to the development of their own personality with all of their attention and strength. When this is the case, it makes sense to direct the unused means to a significant application within the scope of our own development—or we can make them available to others for constructive projects until we really need them again. The more "dead capital" that lies around, the more intensely the owner's development will be impeded by this burden.

So wealth is not an objective quantity, but a subjective quantity. We can be rich with $500 a month and poor with $50,000 a month; it depends on how we live with the means available to us. Once this fact has become totally clear to us, we'll be able to make much more of our lives than we had ever dreamed of.

Why Do People Want to Become Wealthy?

Practically every human being would like to be wealthy, even those who flatly reject the idea at first. Time and again, I have observed that people who praise poverty soon begin to extol wealth—when it becomes attainable for them. But there are a huge variety of motives why we strive for wealth.

The first motive is fear. A great many people would like to call loads of money and possessions their own so that they are protected against the risks of life. They think they can buy a sense of security and protection. However, reality has repeatedly proved the opposite to be true. Those who are rich in the material sense are often the specific targets of all types of terrible crimes. There are many people who would like to take the money and possessions away from a rich person in order to become rich themselves. Moreover, greed, fears, envy, mistrust, and miserliness spread easily when the wealth of a human being is not properly understood and used in the holistic sense. This leads to battles, conflict, and increasingly more fear about our own well-being, which we feel to be constantly threatened. This tendency doesn't particularly contribute to happiness and harmony.

Many people want to become wealthy on the basis of the belief that they can attain a better quality of life as a result. However, these expectations are deceptive as well. In any case, they always are when a person doesn't learn what wealth means in the holistic sense and how it should be sensibly put to use while climbing the ladder of success. Quality of life develops from a loving, thankful soul who knows how to meaningfully use the opportunities of the Creation.

Individuals who would like to be rich in material goods because they believes that this is the only way they will be able to live properly, also fail to see the important experiences that they could have in the presumably "poor" stages of their path in life. So many treasures are within reach for each of us: happy times with true friends, an idyllic sunset, a tasty meal that has been lovingly prepared, a valuable book, sensual experiences with a beloved partner... The list is endlessly long! This wealth is available to everyone, whether millionaire or not. There's so much to learn at each stage of our path. If we want to become wealthy, the best precondition for it is always being open to all the gifts and not looking down on them if we can't immediately turn them into dollars and cents. If we always just stare at the great, distant goal of "wealth," we'll overlook the table full of presents in front of us: In the holistic sense, this is the best precondition for staying poor.

If you desire to become wealthy in the holistic sense, you will find yourself on a truly promising path. I've written this book for you. The other people will soon put it down anyway when they don't find the recipe they expected for becoming a millionaire within a year. However, before we both take a closer look at what natural, holistic wealth is and how it can be used meaningfully, I would like to address one more barrier that stops people from becoming rich or using their wealth in a way that brings blessings.

Why Are People Afraid of Wealth?

When we are rich, we basically have many opportunities. This form of power, of energy, can let all the aspects of our being stand out more intensely. This is like a lamp that has its brightness regulated by a dimmer. If we turn it down and let very little electricity flow, the lamp will only glimmer. If we turn it up, giving it more energy, it will brightly illuminate the room—and the shadows of things that are in the way of the light will stand out more sharply.

The shadow sides within ourselves, the unresolved and unloved aspects of our personality that are always present and yet not understood, will also stand out more intensely because of the increased energy. Power doesn't corrupt, as is often wrongly believed. It only gives the latent corruption an opportunity to become active. Being confronted with this aspect of our own character can be quite frightening. Illusions about our self-image must be abandoned sooner or later and the constructive confrontation with our own shadow, the imaginary demons, *initially* costs a great deal of energy and also is very painful because of the friction with our own resistance.

Afterward, we will naturally feel much better. But this will only be after a relatively long haul. Perhaps we won't be able to see it through and may fall apart because of the demands that exceed our weak powers*? Some friends, who actually never were friends, will probably turn away from us in envy or fear. Will we find new friends or stay behind in loneliness? Who can know the answer to this! Opportunities and risks are always very closely related. If we don't try it out, we will never exactly know whether we are capable of dealing with such a situation or not. However, if we take risks and apply all our strengths, one thing will be certain: We will *always* progress much farther in our personal growth. We will experience what we really have within us, see our possibilities—and our limitations—much more clearly, gather many important experiences, and learn to do new things. Once we have equipped ourselves in this way and have grown, we will make progress with every new attempt. At some point, we will then lose our fear of imaginary failure and recognize that:

The path is the only true goal in the life of a human being.

This attitude, which is realistic in the holistic sense, opens all the doors to happiness and success for us since we can *never lose again.* But how do we now deal concretely with the problems along the way? It should be clear to us that whenever we are challenged, we always have two possibilities: for one thing, we can depend on our strength. Once we have truly found it and trust in it, then there will be a great deal of energy and we will have many abilities that can help us deal with the difficulties that the new learning situations bring with them. Perhaps this will be enough...

---

* *Basically speaking, no one is truly weak. But many people would like to be weak so that they don't have to stand on their own two feet!*

The other choice is to do what is feasible for us. We can ask the creative force to support us in whatever we can't take care of ourselves in order to be successful and get further in life. Perhaps this path may sound somewhat removed from reality, but it has worked well time and again. We must do the best we can to act with a pure heart in the intention of serving the benefit of all participants; in everything else, we can trust in the blessing that we can request from above to perfect our efforts. We will naturally also be afraid that we won't receive some of the things that we absolutely wanted to have and pout about it at first. But the circumstances will be much more helpful to us than we can perhaps imagine right now. If we accept the fruits of our work, whatever they may be, we will later discover that these are often much sweeter and healthier than whatever it was that we originally wanted to have. The universe will take care of us in the optimal way each time, if we only let it!

Go ahead and risk taking the path of natural, holistic wealth. Ultimately, it's the only one that offers us the opportunity of experiencing everything that we can be. It lets us see the fruits of our achievements ripen, cheerfully harvesting them together with others, and enjoying a fulfilled life in the process. If we act in this manner, our experiences will increasingly give us more security and we can, carried along by the flow of universal life energy, develop and apply our talents for the benefit of all beings. In the course of time, fear will lose its threatening nature for us. We will know that we are always given support for our plans. We will never be alone and without friends. We promote the Creation and it reciprocates by supporting us with all its circumspection and powerful forces. If we reach our hands out to the Creator, we will become wealthy.

Remember: "God only enters into equal partnerships!"

Nature and Wealth

Nature promotes life in wealth and abundance. Look at the trees: They draw from their environment, absorbing water, sunlight, minerals, and carbon dioxide. This is how they maintain their lives, growing in breadth and height. And this isn't all—from their surplus, they also give the surrounding world oxygen, steam, their fruits, and, in autumn, there leaves. Bird's nest in their branches and other small animals live beneath their strong roots. Every year, they grow larger and stronger and can do even more for the rest of Creation. This is the wealth of nature!

We can try to translate this image to our own lives and learn to treat the wealth flowing to us in a natural way. We can be like a tree. We can become aware of our opportunities to grow, to learn, and to accept all kinds of useful things. They are present in every second of our life. We are the only person who can keep this wealth away from us. We simply have to do what needs to be done. We can try to make as much as possible out of our abilities and learn to let go of our will to absolutely accomplish or attain certain things at a specific point in time. Being convinced that we already know what we need is the greatest obstacle on the path to wealth. The tree takes what the surrounding world offers. We can orient ourselves toward this idea. There will always be situations in which we have the feeling that things are boring, superfluous, or simply wrong. But somehow we can't get out of them despite all our immediate efforts. This is an important moment for all of us. We should use it and attempt to employ our wide-awake senses to find out what hidden opportunities are waiting for us. They exist—we can be sure of it! At the moment when we meet another human being, make note of certain information, or have a specific experience, we will most likely not yet know the purpose of it. But some time later, the little stones of the mosaic will be joined together and then we will understand...

This natural openness of using what is offered is called WU WEI, intentionless action, in ancient Chinese wisdom. Instead of racking our brains about what mental acrobatics are necessary to reach a presumably desirable goal, we can instead apply the sweat of our minds to finding out how to recognize what crosses our path as quickly as possible. Once we recognize an opportunity, we can use it in an optimal manner. In this way, things will become increasingly better for us and we will be able to achieve much more because the flow of life will help us in all our plans. There is also an appropriate expression for this in Chinese philosophy: moving 1,000 pounds with one ounce. We must naturally apply this one ounce of our own strength in the natural sense, but the rest will be taken care of for us by the omnipresent creative force. It will set the enormous weight of 1,000 pounds into motion.

Wealth and Responsibility

When we recognize and accept wealth in the holistic sense – the strength, power, abundance of knowledge, and perception that is waiting for us—we simultaneously assume a great deal of responsibility. This can place a great burden on us. We can attempt to forget it or act like someone else could assume the responsibility for applying the powers that have been entrusted to us.

The price of greatness is responsibility. (Winston Churchill)

But this doesn't always apply to wealth! We must carefully consider and make our decisions as well as we can, without being absolutely sure that we have all the necessary information or are mature enough to make a conscious choice. Yet, it actually isn't all that difficult to deal with the responsibility that wealth automatically brings with it. We already know the process: We do our best with the intention of benefiting all the participants in the respective situation. We can ask for assistance in this task and trust that help will be given to us. If we suppress the responsibility conferred upon us or attempt to unload it somewhere else, we may lose a great deal of wealth in the short run or even the long run. However, this isn't a tragedy but it will continue until we trust ourselves to accept the responsibility of using the rest.

One way or the other, we will also have to fundamentally confront the topic of responsibility in relationship to our pursuit of wealth. No wonder, since in order to learn the meaningful and secure approach to responsibility, the universe has already sent us everything we need! As long as we don't have a great deal of strength, or power, or knowledge to work with it in a practical way, it's simply impossible to learn how to act responsibly. As we can see, everything comes to us for some reason. Everything has its purpose, which is ultimately always to help us progress a bit further on our path, making us more complete and loving individuals.

Poverty and Responsibility

Yes, this also exists! On the one hand, we can learn in a situation of poverty that we are ultimately the only ones who can help us get out of it. As long as we push the responsibility for our unpleasant situation onto others, we cannot become rich for a longer period of time. We will somehow always be dissatisfied about not having enough opportunities. Only when we recognize that we *are the masters of our lives* (meaning that we are in the position to choose whether we want to go up or down the ladder), will we be mature enough for more responsibility, more strength, more power, and more knowledge. And we can receive all of this through wealth.

A situation of poverty that affects us, no matter in what sense, ultimately can always be attributed to a conscious or unconscious decision that *we* have made. We can make a new decision at any time. If we want to experience wealth, we only need to march in a different direction. If we are serious about our choice, we will receive enough help in order to have our first experiences. However, we must then also accept the consequences of a new learning step (see above). We will develop a different perspective of responsibility and poverty once we have put ourselves in a situation of wealth. Then we will have more reserves than we can use directly for ourselves. Now is the time to give help to others who are still in some type of poverty situation so that they can progress on their own. We know from our own experience, which we hopefully have not suppressed, what a miserable situation it is to be poor.* But be careful! This is not a matter of constantly playing the Good Samaritan. Whatever we give should provide other people with a reasonable opportunity of becoming wealthy in their own way on their own terms. This is our task when we want to make some of our surplus available to others. If they don't make use of it, then it's their business and not ours. Each human being must experience things on his or her own, and the help of another person should make this possible when someone has too little means available to get started. We can compare this situation to the starter of an engine. The starter has the function of starting the combustion engine. But then it has to keep running on its own!

---

* *Do you think this sentence is true?* *"Only a person who has really understood poverty can live a life in true wealth without being destroyed by it."*

Wealth or poverty—both make it possible to develop the ability of being responsible, even though this will be achieved in different ways. Whenever we deal with these themes, we should always take into consideration that every ability wants to be used in a sensible way; every talent not yet put to meaningful use builds up the pressure to develop it.

Misused Wealth

Perhaps you are now asking the justified question of how it could be possible that so much abundance is produced and apparently misused in our world. Isn't there something wrong with the cosmic law? Or is this business with abundance and the entire money concept basically evil?

Neither of these possibilities is correct. For one thing, we human beings have inherited an invaluable gift that is probably responsible for most of the troubles in the world: our freedom to do and not do, to think and feel how and what we want.

Secondly, we have all received specific instructions when entering this level of the Creation: We are meant to have experiences! If we want to halfway comprehend the meaning of the whole situation, we can use our freedom in order to have the experiences in a way that is as light and playful as possible, with a great deal of fun, therefore learning in an effective manner and developing ourselves.

We can work with each other, give meaning to relationships, accomplishing constructive work on a basis of equality together with other people, the rest of the living beings of this world, and the cosmic forces. God seems to favor this decision since people who live according to it generally make a much happier impression, in my experience, than the others who are not willing to work together. Those who frequently feel good, enjoy playing and learning, which means they enjoy life, ultimately have more experiences and can integrate them much better.

But we are never forced to use our freedom in a reasonable and constructive manner. In this possible choice lies the source of awareness, of conscious existence that is clear about being able to act correctly or falsely, and having to bear the consequences either way.

So the possibility fundamentally exists in an imperfect and conscious form of understanding, accepting, loving what is imperfect and wrong on the basis of our own imperfection—and thereby making it perfect. The consciousness of imperfection is also the precondition for the ability to love, to grow and develop as human beings! Both of the above-mentioned basic preconditions can't be changed. We can only change ourselves: you and I and the others. But each of us can only do this on the basis of our own decision. No one can do this for anyone else.

"This all sounds well and good," you may say, "but I know a lot of people who are totally spiritual and poor and others who act like pigs and are stinking rich. But that can't be if the good are rewarded and the bad dispossessed." But that isn't how I meant it. Let's take another brief look at the answer to the issue of misuse and meaningful use of wealth in the holistic sense. Each of us who attempts according to our possibilities to translate our best qualities into action according to our own abilities, is clear about always making mistakes as an imperfect person. This means that somehow leaving the rest of the matter up to "upstairs" is a spiritual act. Examples of this may be politicians, economic leaders, or some others in positions of great power. We may frequently think that these people are just talking rubbish and everything should be done differently. To better explain these circumstances better, here is a little exercise:

Relax by listening to your breathing for a while. When you are completely quiet, imagine one of those people who you think makes the most wrong decisions. Attempt to see him or her as vividly as possible in front of your inner eye. Now, with the help of your powers of imagination, slip into him or her. From the other person's perspective, experience the pressure of responsibility that comes from tasks like securing jobs on a long-term basis while protecting the environment, making sure the company survives on the market, doing justice to the various interests of employee groups, developing useful products and services, presenting these to customers so that they will also buy them, and fulfilling legal conditions. At the same time, from the perspective of this person, also think about your health, your partner's birthday, your own continuing education, hobbies, purchases to be made, and all the other trivial everyday matters. So, now make decisions in a way that is harmful to no one! Then slowly

31

draw yourself back into your own everyday consciousness. Do you understand the message? Good. If not, go ahead and do the exercise again. This time, focus even more on relating to the other person's role!

It is *not* possible to exist and take action perfectly in an imperfect world. But it *is* possible to give our best. We can try to lovingly understand the apparent imperfections in dealing with wealth. This doesn't mean that we should leave them as they are. Instead, we can take the hate out of a relationship. We can initially presume that every other person has good intentions. Then many people will use the opportunity to be better. The worse we judge a person to be, the fewer opportunities we leave him or her to be good. Energies spread and enter into an interaction with the entity at which they are directed. Consider how many kinds of energies are projected at the decision-makers of this world every day. Misuse is always more frequent when the people participating in an action simply don't want to understand each other, therefore opening the door to hatred.

Jesus said: "Love your enemies!" When we love and understand our enemies and can thereby comprehend their motivations, we attain the true opportunity for ourselves to change something for the better in this world. What we love serves us—what we hate opposes us! Everything that we do from a feeling of separation, of misunderstanding, of hate will absorb and circulate the energy that we radiate. For example: Nothing very good can come of it when people demonstrate against nuclear power plants and hate the policemen they are facing, along with the operators of the power plant.*

At different times in their lives, almost all human beings fail to take advantage of their opportunities. As a result, we suffer in some form that corresponds to the intensity of this misuse. This applies even if we play "Mr. Happy" or "Ms. Happy" in public. This misuse always results from the kind of path we are following. No matter how wonderful the goal may be, if we brutally step over dead bodies, in either the figurative or the literal sense, or turn our ego into an idol, our path does not correspond to the law of love (see below). Consequently, we are abusing this law. If our goal is less respected,

---

* *We can learn a great deal from Mahatma Gandhi and his life. If this topic interests you, the "Gandhi" film and many biographies are available.*

but we make the best effort we can, then we act in a spiritual manner and spread the vibration of light. An individual's goal is only of secondary significance: It is more important to observe and understand how he or she follows it. This allows us to comprehend the inner man or woman.

For a human being, the gift of freedom may result in the misuse of wealth. We must always bear the consequences of our freely determined actions. The reward for acting in a spiritual manner as a consequence of the right way to take the personal path can't always be calculated in dollars and cents. Or will anyone who is wise and holy always have a well-filled bank account? The reward is primarily a high quality of life, a life fulfilled in the holistic sense that includes having good, genuine friends. Material wealth can be an expression of this spiritual wealth. However, spiritual wealth may also be expressed in many other ways. These various possibilities will be explained in the next section.

Wealth and the Love-of-Life Chakra

The love-of-life chakra, usually wrongly called the sexual chakra in the related literature, organizes the capabilities of human beings in all types of relationships and, as the fruit of the possible resulting communication, it promotes joy. This is the love of life that can only come from the gut and find fulfillment through a constructive, playful approach to the various expressions of the Creation. Only in relationships do we experience within ourselves our capabilities and shortcomings. Only in the exchange with others do we find genuine emotional fulfillment, a deeper meaning in life.

In the Bible, it states: "It is not good to be alone, which is why God decided to create a companion for man," and anyone can experience the wisdom of this statement in everyday life. What is life without friends and a partner?

I classify wealth with the second chakra. This is the abundance that results from the personal, unique creative power of the individual working together with the vibration of the universal life energy. This is the product of the equal relationship among three parties: God, human beings, and the surrounding world. What develops from this is the precondition for evolution's constructive progression. When this abundance with its special quality (always characterized by the unique abilities of the participating human beings) can be made available to other beings for perfecting their work, the result is an optimal shaping of evolution. It's fun to participate in this event. Seeing beautiful things created on the basis of your own efforts, working together with others, harvesting together and enjoying the abundance, this is fulfilling!

The love of life takes place within the relationship. The simplest example: a child conceived and raised together by a man and woman with the help of the divine power of life is an expression of their mutual love. Consciously experienced, this process is beautiful and fulfilling. It is a process in which abundance is created. Neither of the two participants becomes poorer because of the act of conception. The flow of energies makes everyone richer and lets them learn and grow—if they make use of the opportunity! So three participating parties working together fundamentally create wealth and abundance: the creative force and two representatives of the material world. They are a product of joy in life. Let's participate in the dance of creation and enjoy ourselves!

How You Can Become Unbelievably Wealthy in about 15 Minutes

"Finally, now he's going to give me a tip on how I can quickly become a millionaire!" you may now be thinking. And you're right. I would like to show you a hidden treasure. You can have it all to yourself, if you like. It's so large that all the gold in Fort Knox seems like a welfare check in comparison. Do you want it?

O.K., close your eyes. Let's go on a treasure hunt together, which lasts about 15 minutes. Then you will be wealthy! Try to forget any agitation you may feel and listen to your breathing in order to relax. When you feel quiet and settled, pay attention to your head. Feel the brain within your skull and become aware of what it is: a super computer with unbelievable capacity!

The largest electronics companies in the world fund research with billion-dollar budgets in order to produce megabyte chips, electronic memories. At this very moment, your brain is already accomplishing feats many times more complicated than the next generations of computer chips that are still only on the drawing board. Today, or in the foreseeable future, there is no one in the world capable of building a computer that is even approximately as fast, as versatile, with as great a capacity and yet is so small, self-programming, self-maintaining, transportable, and capable of reproduction as *your brain*. Be aware of the unbelievable abilities of your thinking machine!

Next, direct your attention to your sensory organs. Perceive your eyes, your ears, your sense of touch, your sense of smell and taste, the abilities, the temperature differences, the subtle energies, and the movements of your body. Become aware of the potential of your senses as much as possible. What do you believe a machine with this capacity would cost? Could it even be created at all with the current status of technology?

And now, let's look at your locomotor system: you can run, jump, climb, crawl, swim, dive, bike, walk on your hands, dance, climb stairs, and much, much more! Did you know that scientists remain unsuccessful in their attempt to build a robot that can walk only half as well as a human being! Explore other areas of your body in this way. For example, take a look at the digestive tract, the body's immune system, the reproductive organs, the detoxification capabilities, etc. After this exercise (which you can repeat frequently), try to take this awareness of the enormous wealth you possess back into everyday life with you in order to get a new, more positive perspective on your life.

Don't just pass over this exercise with a condescending smile! It can be the key to lasting success in your life. The more we become aware of the wealth that we have inherited, the better our prospects of becoming successful will be. We represent a species of beings that have been the most successful in asserting themselves of all the forms of life on this planet up to now. You are related to people like Albert Einstein, Socrates, Marie Curie, St. Hildegard of Bingen, Holderlin, Coco Chanel, Buddha, and Jesus. All of these people brought the same attributes as you have with them into this world. So don't back out now and try to lie to yourself that they were different in some way. These people were just conscious of their potential. In the last exercise, you just achieved a small degree of this kind of consciousness. And they used their potential by awakening it, trying it out, and thereby developing it. Now it's your turn! Use your treasures well!

Key Principles for an Approach to Your Wealth that Creates Happiness

1. The law of love

When we spread the vibration of love through our freely determined thoughts and actions, trying to the best of our ability to have a constructive impact beneficial to all those involved, we have the opportunity of receiving return service from the universe in the form of holistic wealth.

2. The law of unbiased acceptance

If we take what the universe gives us instead of attempting to assert our will and achieve something very specific outside of our momentary range, we will become wealthy in the holistic sense. What we receive will always be optimally tailored to our true needs in terms of the amount and quality.

3. The law of path and goal

If we walk our path consciously and playfully, while learning and spreading love, our lives will be filled with meaning and we will become rich. If our attention is constantly focused on a specific goal to the point that we no longer perceive the process of progressing on our path as the main issue, we will remain poor in the holistic sense. When we reach the goal of our lives, we can only receive what we have collected along our life's path!

Chapter 3

THE SPIRITUAL MEANING
OF WORK

A person is young when he believes he must work; he is mature,
when he hopes to be allowed to work; and he is old when he is
thankful for still being able to work.
(Ron Kritzfeld)

Before I go into detail about *my* views on the meaning of work,
I would like to give you the opportunity to become aware of your
own ideas on this subject. After all, this chapter is about work – so,
let's go!

What Work Means for You—
A Little Character Study

Without giving it much thought (this is very important!), please
complete the following sentences:

When I think of **work,** the first thing that occurs to me is ....

....

To me, **leisure** means ....

When I **work,** I'm frequently overcome by a feeling of ....

....

When the **end of the working day** approaches, I often feel ....

....

The **meaning** of my life is ....

I **work** because I ....

Right now, don't think about these statements anymore. Put them aside and look at them again after one day, three days, and seven days. Each time you do this, write down your resulting feelings with honesty and as much detail as possible.

Now let's focus on the distribution of work and leisure in your life.

I spend about ....hours a week working.

I spend about ....hours a week with leisure activities (don't include sleep!)

I spend about ....hours a week sleeping.

Look at the distribution of your time. If you like how you use your time, write a few sentences to say why. Look at these reasons again after one day, three days, and seven days. Focus each time on what you feel and write down your perceptions in keywords, but not in a superficial way. If you don't like the division of your time, explain to yourself (as if you were talking to a good friend) why and how the distribution of your time could be arranged in a way that is more appealing to you. When you have ended this exercise, again put your statements aside for one week. Then reread them, focus on yourself, and write down your feelings about them.

Write down 15 terms that are connected with the word "**work**" for you.

Write down 15 terms that are connected with the word "**leisure**" for you.

For each of the 30 terms, now put down a "+" if you rate it in an emotionally positive way and a "—" if you rate it in an emotionally negative way. A neutral rating isn't permissible since it would then be too easy to hide. In which of the two groups do you show an overall more positive evaluation? If someone had asked you beforehand which area you rate more positively, would your response have been similar? If you consciously prefer one of the two areas of life, it should be clear to you that the other area, which also represents a part of you, is being neglected. Do you really want this situation? If not, why are you doing this to yourself? And if so, are you really aware of all the consequences involved in living your life this way—even the long-term consequences? Think about this for a while and take a look at your feelings. Jot down your perceptions so that you can go through them again at a later time. When you refer back to them, do you discover any changes in your attitude? If yes, which changes?

Let's take a look at the roles you have created for yourself in your various life situations!

Who are **you** when you **work** (about 10 sentences)?

Who are **you** when you have **leisure time** (about 10 sentences)?

Now try to reduce each of these 10 sentences to one or two core statements about your roles in order to get a clearer picture of what your two masks look like. Write down what you would tell your best friend if she had made these statements about herself and then asked you for your comments.

O.K., Enough self-analysis! Let's now take a closer look at the spiritual dimension of work.

What Does Work Mean in the Esoteric Sense?

In esotericism, work means an activity that offers people developmental opportunities when they confront its demands and participate in the process of a holistically meaningful exchange of energy with others. In this exchange, we have the opportunity to adjust to other people's needs, satisfy them according to their capabilities, and accept the energy qualities that we basically can't develop ourselves or would be forced to neglect other needs that are essential for us if we did.

Strenuous and Relaxing Activities

Work can be done in a relaxing and meditative manner or it can make us tense and agitated. Which of these alternatives a person experiences is a decision made by the respective individual! This may perhaps sound a bit heretical to you, but many people all over the world succeed in doing their work in a relaxed and meditative manner. However, many others feel exhausted instead of pleasantly tired like a child who has played dynamically and expressed enthusiasm and joy. What is the actual reason for this? What makes work meditative and what causes it to be stressful and exhausting? How can we learn to experience work as meditation?

The previous section took the spiritual perspective that work is fundamentally a significant and indispensable opportunity for learning and growing. Through it, we can experience the surrounding world and ourselves. Every time that we learn something, we must naturally let go of old, familiar attitudes that are now outdated in order to accept something new. It's always like jumping into cold water when we risk giving up something old and then getting accustomed to other attitudes and having to solve the tasks that life presents. The more we learn, the more responsibility we will assume. This can create fear. And our limitations will become clearer to us—the things that we just cannot do. Frequently, the perception of our own inability in relation to mastering certain demands triggers a feeling of helplessness, at least momentarily. Fears about terrible consequences, like being fired, not getting a promotion, losing your image, and so forth, begin to grow. As a result, we experience our own limitations and gradually perceive that we are dependent upon the help of others and need to trust enough to let go. This is a good breeding ground for basic anxiety! Most of the processes described in this way take place beneath the surface of waking consciousness. When we work and are simultaneously forced to repeat experiences that trigger our subconscious mind's response to our fears, flight reactions and the creation of readiness for action, this is negative stress. Our root chakra becomes active and attempts to secure our survival. On the other hand, our conscious mind knows precisely that it isn't permitted to flee or openly fight with work colleagues. After all, we have committed ourselves to accomplishing a specific job and are dependent upon the salary or other results of working. This is quite a dilemma, isn't it? One solution to this tricky problem that has functioned well time and again is to learn to do our work consciously. This means noticing our own resistance to it, accepting it, and understanding* its meaning in order to be able to let go of it and make way for new experiences. In this manner, we are no longer helplessly at the mercy of your resistance. Our conscious approach to it gives us the opportunity to get the flaws out of our character, slowly but surely. There is also an appropriate name for this type of work:

---

* This type of healing naturally also takes place in the three steps of "truth," "love," and "perception." Also compare this approach to the comments in my books "Aura Healing Handbook" and "The Complete Reiki Handbook".

ZEN Work

The ZEN path is a Japanese form of Buddhism, which originally developed in India. It has influenced broad areas of art and culture, martial arts, and the general attitude toward life in Japan. One of its core sentences is: "Consciousness is everything!" This means that only a conscious approach to life opens up the possibility of change. What we don't perceive, we can't change. And, this is perhaps even more important: The more consciously we are involved in what we are doing, the less we will experience ourselves as being foreign and separate. With every action, we create unity within ourselves and with the world. This alone causes many fears, points of friction, and boundaries that we have set for ourselves to disappear! Our entire personality, everything that we are, therefore exists within our actions. Tremendous energies are triggered in this way. This is the secret of karate fighters and kung fu experts, who can split several concrete plates or blocks of ice with a single blow of their hands, which are made of flesh and blood just like your own, and not even hurt themselves in the process! The conscious direction of all their energies into this blow makes it possible for them to do tasks that seem quite fantastic. Yet, they are absolutely not supermen (or superwomen), but are just making proper, natural use of their human abilities. Today, many managers are being trained in the ZEN path in order to better complete their assignments and do so with less wear-and-tear. Top athletes practice it in order to achieve maximum performance. But each and every one of us, even you, can access the proper, natural use of our own abilities by working consciously and devoting ourselves to our job. Simply start by meditating. Initially, you may have a difficult time doing it. Yet, because of your good experiences with this path, you will probably receive so much confirmation that it will become increasingly easier for you. Limitations that you have set for yourself will gradually fall away. New, unimagined possibilities will open up to you. This is what you will experience when you have trust in yourself and take this new path.

Worshippers of Leisure and Workaholics

There are essentially two basic attitudes toward work in our society. First, there are the *workaholics,* these are the poor souls who drudge and slave as much as they can and would like to do even more, if possible. If you ask why they do so much, they will answer with conviction, each in his or her own way, that there is absolutely no other approach to doing things. Of course, this is nonsense, as anyone who has seen more of the world and doesn't identify with this approach can discover. But it's a part of the fight for survival, being imprinted with strong fear patterns to agilely maneuver yourself into a blind alley and then to resist with all your might the desire to march back out again.

The other extreme are the worshippers of leisure who think that work is an evil that sometimes can't be avoided, but real life takes place during leisure time are the other extreme. They attempt to work as little as possible, fighting primarily for less and less work hours with increasingly more pay. Vacation time is the most precious season of the year for them. With this negative attitude toward work, they naturally carelessly miss out on important learning situations and opportunities for development. By virtually declaring that portions of their lives are insignificant, they lose a great deal of meaning in life. How unfortunate! It's no wonder that with this state of mind they have ultimately created for themselves, these people suffer from their work and can't perceive much joy in developing their own opportunities, which include confirming their sense of self-worth and experiencing their selves in an energy-providing manner.

So what actually are the causes for the misuse of work and leisure? Both disharmonies basically can be traced back to the same root: fear. In the case of *workaholics*, work is a type of anesthetic that prevents them from waking up and becoming involved with themselves. If we watch someone who is addicted to work, we get the impression of seeing a machine. And this is exactly what they want to be, a well-oiled machine that never fails and is therefore always needed. Their justification for living is their good work. Behind this stance lurks the fear of not being loved when they are no longer needed, being defeated and dying if they cease to constantly struggle.

This is ultimately the primitive fear of being lonely, deserted, and separate. The proponents of leisure avoid the confrontation with work because within the depths of their souls they fear failure, not doing justice to what is required of them, and being helplessly lost in fulfilling the goal to be achieved. Moreover, here we find the primitive fear of being separate, helplessly at someone else's mercy, and constantly having to fight in order to survive. This battle tends to be expressed in a passive attitude of refusal. Trying to basically understand both forms of misusing areas of life is quite useful. We can also find these blocks within ourselves. When we work on them, we become free to be who we really are.

Of course, work and leisure are both important and necessary. They mutually complement and support each other when they are correctly understood, lived in a conscious manner, and enjoyed. The law of yin and yang says that everything in life consists of polarities. Harmony exists as long as a free, natural interchange of the yin and yang forces takes place and both are represented in an approximately equal manner. Work is classified with the active, creative principle of the yang energy; leisure is part of the passive, receptive pole of the yin force. Cheerful, conscious working with all the available powers and gathering experiences must be complemented with phases of rest in a meaningful and balanced relationship. This permits us to regenerate the powers and digest our experiences, serving to integrate the new contents into our own structures. When we have eaten well, which can also be classified with the yang principle, we should rest for a while in order to make the strength available for the digestion of the food. There certainly needs to be an opportunity for the body to gather its resources in the abdomen for digestion purposes after a meal. We become tired and reduce our activities. As a result, the body is given a good opportunity to digest the food and assimilate it into the metabolism.

We can learn to use both of these phases equally, which will enormously increase our quality of life. In keeping with the group to which we tend toward, resistance of many types will naturally arise. We must learn to deal with it.

We can approach our work in a conscious way and use the opportunities inherent to it. This acquaints us with the joy that lies in dynamic self-fulfillment. Every day, we can be aware of everything that we have created. We can notice how the products of our work enrich the lives of others, and what we were able to learn as a result. Our times of rest will be much more satisfying than before when we can let ourselves sink into the pleasant tiredness that automatically occurs after a time of intense, satisfying activity.

We can throw ourselves into our phases of rest as intensively as into our work and surrender to the sweet feeling of doing nothing. And then we really shouldn't be involved with anything that could somehow strain us. If we can't accept this approach too well at the beginning, we can comfort ourselves with the thought that the time of work will automatically come again. We will notice that we can work much more effectively and easily when we have made intensive use of resting phases.

We may be pleasantly surprised to find that, through this type of life style, many of the psychosomatic complaints that we currently have will disappear and the others will drastically improve. We can now bring harmony into our life by consciously balancing the yin and yang forces. It's also obvious that this approach will have a beneficial effect on our health!

Work as a Path to Self-Fulfillment

We experience ourselves within the process of working. Our possibilities become increasingly clear to us through the constant application of our strengths and the search for solutions. In the same way, we will also reach our limitations time and again. Sometimes we may be able to move beyond them and increase our strengths. But we may often recognize that certain boundaries are based on our constitution and simply can't be overcome. We can learn to accept and love these boundaries as an important part of our selves. They assume the function of channeling our energy. They assist us in more clearly seeing our tasks in life when we accept their help. This is because when we don't do things that we are simply unsuited for in terms of our abilities, we can concentrate on what is right for us. This makes it much easier. We then have more success, but—and this is far more important, this is how we gather the experiences that largely correspond with our life plan. Before we were born into this world, we precisely considered the red thread that would run through this new incarnation. We put together our genetic traits accordingly, looked for the most suitable family, and then things started happening! Even if this idea may not be the most appealing, it can teach us to consciously accept responsibility for our lives.

The more we recognize our abilities and limitations, finding and accepting ourselves as a result, the more playful and cheerful our approach to work situations will be. We will then quickly know whether or not something is suitable for us and can act accordingly. Fears of failure and inferiority complexes will gradually disappear once we have experienced our own talents time and again. This will strengthen our self-confidence. Then it will no longer be so terrible if there is something we can't do. Then we just forget it and do what we can do, gathering experiences in the process. People who have experienced and found themselves through their work radiate an inner cheerfulness, self-assurance, and warmth. They have accepted themselves and therefore learned the lesson of self-love. They are no longer in conflict with themselves and the world since there is peace and quiet in their hearts. And this stillness is the mother of strength.

Work and Love

If we use work as a type of self-realization, we will continue to get closer to ourselves. The closer we get to the essence of our being, the more our heart chakra will open. Truly getting to know something, experiencing and understanding it in all its forms of expression, allows us to learn to love it. If we love ourselves with all our rough edges, merits and talents, then we can also leave others as they are. The fighting and competition are useless since every human being has unique talents. If we become familiar with our talents, learn to love and use them meaningfully, then there is no one who can surpass us in our own sphere, because each of us is unique!

Competition only occurs when people don't live out their uniqueness; instead, they play around on the same field as others like amateurs. In order to assert themselves, they must then lower the prices of their goods and services in a disproportionate manner, work more,

46

advertise intensively, and suffer a lot of stress. When lower prices appear to be the best sales argument, there will always be someone else who has something better to offer: namely, even lower prices. Unique services are always worth the money because, as a result of their high quality, they can fulfill an important function for the customer's lifestyle. This is why people who achieve self-fulfillment in their work in a loving manner are always the most successful in the long run. If we want to learn to live in a loving way, then we must begin with our work. Particularly here, where most people presumably think it would be least likely, we can most easily open our heart chakra and experience that self-fulfilled love makes us wealthy and happy in life.

Work and the Power Chakra

A further treasure lies hidden in the conscious approach to work: the harmonious development of the 3rd energy center, the power chakra. When we approach the challenges of our work consciously and lovingly, we can constantly continue to develop our ability to solve problems by first thinking about them. Then we can design situations so that we are able to deal with them, process information, and influence others to our advantage from the perspective of holistically meaningful goals. We will also learn to draw the line at inappropriate demands in a harmonious and natural way to save our strengths for more meaningful activities.

Does this power frighten you? Or are you totally curious about it? Whatever your situation may be, your blocks, since fear and greed are blocks—will automatically be healed when you learn to approach your working situation in a loving way. The heart chakra (responsible for love and acceptance) and the power chakra (responsible for manipulation and drawing the line) will complement and mutually promote each other in their development when you consciously use your abilities. Love united with power can accomplish wonderful things. Love without power is helpless, power without love is destructive.

Key Principles for an Approach to Our Work
That Creates Happiness

1. The law of consciousness

Everything that we do consciously will ultimately have a healing and fulfilling effect upon us. Everything that we do unconsciously will ultimately not advance our progress in life.

2. The law of self-fulfillment through self-expression

Self-expression is absolutely necessary for self-fulfillment since we experience ourselves in our works. In their uniqueness, we can recognize our own uniqueness as individuals.

3. The law of harmonious lifestyle

Only when activity is complemented by inactivity in a balanced manner do our talents develop in a holistic and harmonious manner. Just as digestion is part of eating, the gathering of experiences through activity is necessarily and naturally complemented by their integration during passivity.

It is important to apply these laws in order to become and remain holistically wealthy.

Chapter 4

The Spiritual Meaning of an Occupation

What Is the Esoteric, Hidden Meaning of an Occupation?

The term "occupation" is related to the term "calling." In ancient times, a person's "social class and position" were seen as a divine task in the world. People's occupations were meant to reflect their spiritual calling, corresponding to their life plan. Today, most people have a much more profane concept of these terms: an occupation should bring enough money to live, not be a burden, and have a good image. This chapter explores how important it is to follow a personal calling in your occupation. People would be somewhat happier if they would find and accept their assignment in life. At the same time, fulfilling the calling represents an inestimable contribution to the harmonious evolution of the Creation.

The true occupation of a human being is to find himself!
(Hermann Hesse)

As human beings, each of us is unique and our own respective talents can't be replaced by anyone else. Yet, how can we live our calling in modern times, where everyone is more or less put into inappropriate categories? How can we find it at all? Here are some effective means for achieving this.

The Choice of an Occupation and Opening the 3rd Eye

The third eye is the term used for an energy center located in the middle of the forehead, approximately at the level of our eyebrows.

It has the function of perception, of helping us to find our path. Through its abilities, we can learn to comprehend our personal plan in life. But what actually is this life plan?

Before we were born into this world, we decided upon a certain constitution and starting situation. This choice was made according to the requirements of our personal life plan. It contains all the areas in which we want to gather experiences in the new incarnation. Specific processes are rarely exactly defined in terms of time. By the same token, the kinds of experiences that we have with specific partners also aren't usually precisely determined. We decide for the most part about the course of our life, about happiness and unhappiness, success and failure. The most important thing is that certain areas are touched upon and the result is learning the contents. Consequently, we integrate them as well as possible. The more consciously we attune ourselves to our "red thread," the easier our life will be. This attunement is possible in a number of different ways. Here are two good possibilities for finding out the nature of our calling:

Exercise 1: The Amethyst Perception Exercise

This method can be used frequently to repeatedly attune yourself to the fine energy patterns of your path in life. Prepare for the exercise in the following way: Find a good-quality amethyst about the size of a walnut that has been tumbled into a round shape. Energetically cleanse it for about 30 seconds under cold, flowing water. Then go to a quiet place in which you feel good and secure. Sit down comfortably and listen to the flow of your breathing until you are calm and relaxed. Now hold the healing stone with both hands in front of your third eye, which is located at the center of your forehead between your eyebrows. Then say; "I open myself for the perception-enhancing power of this crystal and ask for the blessing and protection of the cosmic forces of light and love so that I may fulfill my calling." Stay in contact with the stone for some time, at least 10 minutes. Consciously surrender to its guiding vibration. To end the exercise, lower the crystal again, look at it, and thank it for its help. Also thank the forces of light and love. Then take a few deep breaths and look around you to once again establish contact with the world of everyday life.

Exercise 2: A Trip into Your Childhood

This method can help you establish contact with the original plans for your occupation—your calling. Only do the exercise at larger time intervals of at least 14 days and take notes on your experiences afterward.

Each of us still had a good connection with our third eye as a small child. This small child with big astonished eyes, who looks forward to living its uniqueness in this world and enriching others with it, is still within you. Once again, look for a quiet place that appeals to you and gives you a sense of security when you take your journey to your inner child. Get comfortable and listen to your breathing for a while in order to relax your body and mind. Close your eyes and go further and further back into your childhood. Take your time and open up to the memory of important stages of your life. Allow yourself to daydream a little bit while you do this, but always return to the route of your journey. Press further back to the time of your youth, then your childhood, until you remember situations that took place at some time between the ages of three and six years. You can extend this inner journey according to your mood. But nothing substantial will take place if you do it for less than 15 minutes. In any case, you should invest at least this much time. It may be that you need several attempts so that you can clearly call to mind your experiences at this age.

Perhaps between the exercises you can look at photos from this period of your life or talk to relatives, acquaintances, and old friends about your childhood. Perhaps you may also start becoming a bit more childlike and playing more. Have the courage to enjoy it. All of this can contribute to mobilizing your memories, awakening your inner child, and letting it express itself. Be patient, it will happen after a time, and then you can access this stage of life from your memory whenever you want. Now search for situations in which you expressed a preference for certain occupations, professions, and paths in life. Try to particularly remember those that had little or nothing to do with your parents' path in life. Go back a number of times until you have a confident feeling about what your wishes were at that time. These are very rarely concrete ideas about an occupation, but tend instead to deal with *how* you wanted to take up these professions. At some point, you will know precisely what was going on inside of you back then. Trust yourself and take this knowledge back into the adult world with you. Live it! The more you translate it into reality in your everyday life, the more you will understand and experience what it means to have a calling.

In addition to this, but only in addition, you can also work with some sort of oracle based on synchronicity like the Tarot or the I Ching in order to become aware of your calling and actively live it. A good astrologer can also give you some important suggestions on the basis of your horoscope.

Practicing Your Occupation and Awakening Your Expression Chakra

Through the realization of our calling, we receive the opportunity of expressing ourselves as we are. This ability is organized by the 5th chakra, the throat energy center. Everything that we do ultimately has its roots within us. It may be that these roots don't extend very deep and are actually just based more or less on good repetition of the forms of expression that we have learned by heart. If this is so, then our self-expression will never be truly satisfying since in reality we are expressing someone else's energy. Our self-confidence isn't strengthened as a result, on the contrary, it tends to be diminished. However, if we learn to find and use the deep roots of our ability to express ourselves, our unique talents in the abundance of our creative activity will be revealed and become a blessing for the world and us.

Key Principles for an Approach to Your Occupation that Creates Happiness

1. The law of unique calling

No one else is in the position to do what we can do if we accept what we truly are within the essence of our selves. The talents concealed there are valuable for everyone and are absolutely unique.

2. The law of flexible self-fulfillment

Time and again, the flow of life brings us back to new situations that are appropriate for us and conceived for the purpose of revealing further areas of our talents. We shouldn't cling to any stages of our life. We can follow the flow of the energy and always try to achieve self-fulfillment in the best, most unique way possible in the situations arising in our lives. When necessary, we can bend like the bamboo reed in the storm wind, while staying firmly rooted in our own energy. Every storm will pass. If we remain flexible within it, we will always come out of every challenge strengthened and with more maturity.

3. The law of the living example

If we want to learn how to be ourselves, we should orient ourselves toward people who live their uniqueness more than we do. Even if they may initially seem quite exotic and incomprehensible to us, we should be respectful and open for what they have to give us through their living example. If we are on our path and achieve self-fulfillment on our own largely through what we do, we should recognize our responsibility to help other people who are seeking to find their own individual strength and personal path. Even if they may initially appear to be uncomprehending and banal to us, we can set a living example for them. As a result of this teaching activity, we will increasingly awaken more talents within ourselves and also be able to continue learning. We should treat our students with respect and gratitude since we are ultimately playing the same game as they are, but in different roles. Perhaps a student will also become our teacher in certain situations. But we can be open to this and accept what is offered.

Chapter 5

THE SPIRITUAL MEANING OF POSSESSIONS

What Is the Esoteric Meaning of Possessions?

The concealed dimension of possessions lies in the unique possibility of participating in the Creation by dealing with them in a responsible manner. This means being capable of designing, developing, and connecting a piece of the world with the rest of the universe in a meaningful way through a divine commission, but under our own direction. The conscious approach to our possessions can help us better understand the role of God and bring us closer to God in the process. According to many old traditions, humans were created in God's image. But do we truly recognize the part of our self that is divine, intact, and whole? On this level, we all have the task of perceiving the spark of divinity in our material shells, learning to love it, and letting its light shine brightly into the world. Then it can connect with many other little lights and ultimately merge with the great light of the elemental force of Creation into a synthesis that transcends the cosmic consciousness. Possessions can help us discover our own strength as a creator and preserver, develop it, and therefore learn to live these divine aspects.

Possessions and Grounding

Possessions are a portion of the earth assigned to us, and they connect us with it. They can be our grounding, the source of our yin energy. By augmenting, protecting, and learning to use them in an increasingly better manner, the value of the earthly quality is formed within our consciousness. When we experience what kind of wonderful possibilities the earth offers us, our respect for material things will grow and at some point turn into sincere love. Possessions connect us with material existence, the yin pole of the life energy.

You can't truly understand something if you haven't possessed it at least once—and you can't truly possess something if you haven't understood it at least once.

Our original, innermost possession is our body, the seat of our soul. When we get older, we receive further, more external possessions in keeping with necessity and our openness for the gifts of the universe. We can lose these again through a great variety of situations in life. We only give up our body when our earthly existence has ended. A further form of possessions is food, water, and air. They belong to us at times, and then they leave us again when they have fulfilled their purpose for us in the cycle of energies. In their quick circulation, they basically reflect what other, more external possessions do at a much slower rate. The air that we breath makes itself available to us so that our metabolism functions and can assimilate energy and eliminate certain toxins, meaning substances that are unusable for us. These are not *used up*—destroyed—but rather *used* in that they enter into many relationships with other substances within us, end these again, and ultimately leave us in order to serve other beings. So we need them to develop our abilities and maintain our physical state.

If, for example, we have a car, a different external possession, this basically fulfills the same tasks. It helps us in the process of our self-fulfillment because with it we can quickly reach important factors in our life like a job, friends, and vacation destinations, and it also protects us from the elements. Possessions are therefore necessary in order to be capable of having experiences. The more we accept them, the better their service to us can be. The more we love them (and this doesn't mean being attached to them), the less it will be possible for us to misuse them for destructive purposes!

Possessions and Responsibility

Everything that we own can be a source of strength and power. Possessions can create wealth and abundance when they are used properly. However, they can also be abused in order to exploit us and our surrounding environment in an unnatural way for absurd goals. Ultimately, we decide how to use our possessions. We can grow as a result of this responsibility, or we can choose not to grow by acting like we are being forced by external circumstances to invest our means in a different manner than we instinctively knows we should.

Possessions bestow power. Power obligates to exemplariness. When the powerful person no longer complies with this obligation, the masses will grab at his possessions. (Moser)

If we want to know how to deal responsibly and holistically with our possessions, we should try to understand why we call a particular possession our own at the moment. What contribution could it make to the development of our self, and how we could use it so that it has the most constructive effect for the world with as little effort as possible? Always primarily imagine the practical goals. The benefit must be concrete. Only then can we check to see how effective and sensible the way we deal with our property is, find possibilities of improvement, and try these out.

Possessions and Love

It is also necessary to love our possessions because everything we love ultimately becomes our helper. Perhaps we sometimes have difficulty in loving our possessions. If so, we can do the following exercise occasionally, which should also be helpful in using our material goods in a holistically sensible and effective manner:

Exercise 1—What Your Possessions Can Do for You

Relax by paying attention to your breathing. Then search your memory for some specific possession of yours. Now become aware of what functions this possession fulfills in your life, how it serves you. Try to recall everything about it as completely as possible. When you think that you've called everything to mind, thank yourself for giving yourself this opportunity. This part of the exercise will help you develop the ability of being grateful, conscious, and able to love.

Then look for all the different ways that you could also use this possession. What services could it offer that you might have previously overlooked? Utilize its possibilities as fully as possible. They are meant for you and waiting for you to finally use them. This part of the exercise will help you use your possessions in a better and more complete way instead of letting them rot away unused in the closet.

Possessions as Obstacles to Development

Whenever we accumulate possessions without making sensible use of them in the holistic sense or either consciously or unconsciously rejecting them, they can impede our development. There is an effective method for avoiding both of these pitfalls, which we already became familiar with in the last section. (If you haven't tried it out yet, think about why you prefer to not use your possessions, like this book.)

Here is a further method worth recommending:

Exercise 2: Throwing Off the Ballast

Take at least one good hour for this exercise. Have paper and something to write with. Go through your living space and gather together those possessions of yours that you no longer need. Carry what you've found to one place and sort it into two piles: one for things that you can sell or give away. These are unnecessary for you, but they may be quite useful to someone else. Make a second pile of things that you want to throw away because in your opinion they no longer have any practical value. Thank both piles of things for their service in your life before you get rid of them. When you have cleared out your living area in this way, burn a little bit of sage everywhere in order to the dispel old energies and make room for all kinds of new things.

Possessions as Turbochargers for Your Development

Properly used, material goods can enormously promote the development of our personality. How does this happen? It's quite simple: With the help of a pendulum and the tables in Appendix 1, or with the chakra-oriented oracle in Appendix 2, find out which chakras primarily need to be developed. Then use the included blank pendulum tables and note the various forms of property that you have. For example: your body, your apartment or house, your garden or yard, books, the television set, the kitchen, painting materials, sports equipment, writing utensils, etc. Now use the pendulum to determine which of your possessions are currently suitable for developing the chakras that need development at this time. Then carry out Exercise 1 described above to find out about all the things you could do with these items. Make a game of it and use the possibilities with a feeling of joy.

Whatever You Inherit from Your Parents, Earn It in Order to Possess It!

There is a deep truth concealed in this phrase. We can't really use something as a possibility for personal growth that we haven't acquired through our own personal efforts until we develop an inner relationship to it and thereby respect, cherish, and love it through the profound understanding of its value. This relationship can only be created from the experiences we have lived and understood, which have grown from the conscious use of the inherited possessions. We should use an intensive and attentive approach to possessions that didn't come to us as the result of our achievements and experience their special quality. Otherwise, they will become ballast.

Seen in a superficial way, inherited assets can certainly give a person an easy, good life. But remember: This doesn't automatically give us meaning, satisfaction, and happiness. To the contrary! If we aren't mindful, we will possibly attempt to avoid the challenges to learn by using the possessions that have been given to us. We may cushion the difficulties that it would be better to overcome and therefore block important opportunities of getting to know our true talents and limitations.

Unused possessions can contribute to a state of unawareness. This applies particularly when we haven't developed an inner relationship to its value and the responsibility connected with the right to use it. This situation naturally not only applies to inherited possessions, but also to every type of asset that comes to us without our personal achievement. It is obvious that such possessions are a great bonus for us if we use them properly from the start. We can discover their value by using them consciously and lovingly, thereby making them our own. This is precisely why these possessions came to us through the favor of the cosmic forces. But, as you know: the greatest opportunities simultaneously bear the greatest risk within them, and vice versa. So let's be happy about them, play lovingly with them, and grow through them!

Possessions and the Rising of the Kundalini Energy

The kundalini energy is the strongest form of polarized energy existent on the earth. This energy is absolutely yin. It is the holy power of the great Mother Earth, whose ultimate purpose it is—carried by the awakened vibration of the human heart—to unconditionally love everything that exists. It is able to rise up to the heavens, the source of the absolute yang energy, and merge with the cosmic consciousness of perception. Contained in our root chakra beneath the coccyx (base of the spine), it waits for us to learn to love earthly existence extensively. Once we have succeeded in doing this, it rises up through the subtle energy channels that connect the chakras with each other, inundating our body and mind with an unbelievable amount of energy. The result is that we can use all the things that we have so strenuously acquired by working for them, for both our further development and for the world since nothing functions without energy. Not even the best engine in the world runs without fuel.

And so that our engine can run at full speed and we can therefore create the possibility of spreading love in the world for ourselves, we receive the gift of the kundalini energy at the appropriate point in time.

It naturally isn't all that easy to learn to love the world in every respect. However, this is possible through the conscious, holistic way of dealing with possessions. Practically as a representative of the entire world, we take a small part of it and attempt to develop a sincere inner relationship and a deep understanding of it. Since all other parts are contained as information in each individual portion of the world, just like the blueprint of our entire body exists within every cell of our organism, we can learn to love and comprehend the whole world in this manner. Once we have progressed well in learning to love, our kundalini will make itself felt so that things can go on from there.

Great, isn't it? And it's much more practical than turning over every individual grain of sand. But even with this possibility, each of us needs diverse rebirths in order to master the task. After all, we can rest in between times on the subtle planes, drink a whisky sour, and go into raptures about the good, old times on the distant earth before we work out a new part of our comprehensive life plan in a different body.

See you!

Key Principles for an Approach to Possessions that Creates Happiness

1. The law of holography

Within each part of the world, the remaining portions are reflected as well. If we learn to absolutely love one part by possessing it and dealing with it in a responsible manner, we will learn to love the entire world.

2. The law of responsibility

Our possessions and their use are our responsibility. If we take advantage of them in the right way, our dealings with the parts of the material world that belong to us will become the engine of our development. If we declare ourselves to not be responsible for them or misuse this gift, our development will be impeded or made impossible.

3. The law of conscious taking and giving

We should expect our possessions to support our personal growth and pay careful attention to their messages. If we receive new goods in addition to what we already have, we should try to understand and accept their function within our life plan. If we must give up possessions, we should try to comprehend which cycle of development has now come to an end for us or where we have resolutely refused to learn so that these possibilities have now had to be diverted to others who want to make more of them. When we accept the end of one learning cycle and keep our eyes open for the next one, we can continue to consciously swim along in the flow of life and succeed in our earthly existence.

Chapter 6
THE MEANING OF EXCHANGE

As soon as we deal with money, an occupation, work, or possessions, all types of exchange processes take place. But stop! Does this only happen in these situations? What about the air we inhale and exhale? Or how about the food that we take in and the substances that are unusable for our body, which we then eliminate and which serve the plants as fertilizer, for example? Or how about what we learn, taking it in, transforming it, and then applying it, giving it back to the outside world? These are all exchange processes! Everything that lives is involved in the process of metabolization: it absorbs substances, makes use of them, and then emits them in a changed form. However, these are not depleted, but others can then assimilate these substances or energies in this particular new form. Exchange is nature, life, and health. In modern holistic medicine, the term "block" is used for something that promotes or causes a health disorder. When the flow of energies and substances is blocked, meaning reduced or completely stopped, illness automatically arises. Standstill is death. An uninhibited interplay of the forces produces life, healing, and growth.

Once we have developed the ability of directing our attention to the flow of energies, noticing where it's not inhibited—and where and why it becomes sluggish or stagnates—these two powers will automatically develop in the process: the power of love and the resulting power of healing. No human being can truly consciously observe death, illness, and suffering for a longer period of time without developing the desire to help, to heal, and to re-establish the state of liveliness since this observation touches the core of our souls, which have come into the world to grow and learn to love. In the final analysis, cruelty is caused by a lack of consciousness. Love will ultimately grow from the frequent, conscious participation in the life processes.

This book is dedicated to the material expression of the Creation because it represents an opportunity for growth and a possibility of enlightenment that is constantly available to every human being. Further down, there will be a more precise explanation of how experiences of enlightenment occur through a conscious exchange with the surrounding world on all levels of existence. However, in order to make this concept easier to understand we need to back up a bit.

The Seven Cosmic Laws of the Creation's Perfection

The continued development of the Creation takes place according to certain eternal laws. In order to guarantee a constant growth and a continual perfection of all life, there must be guidelines such as the basic laws of nature that adequately take all the possibilities into consideration. Even after researching various fields of knowledge and experience with regard to this topic, I don't expect to present perfect solutions without any possibilities of contradiction. Take my carefully evaluated experiences as a suggestion for developing your own perspective on these laws—or accept my conclusions once you have thoroughly examined and found them to be acceptable and applicable in the practical sense. But in any case, please don't simply skip over this important topic and cling to your old opinions. You might miss out on an important opportunity for bringing more meaning, happiness, and success into your life.

The first law says that life is only possible on this level for a being when it participates in the processes of exchange and transformation. The more a being limits these processes, the more it will suffer. In the extreme case, it dies if it fundamentally and lastingly refuses to participate in the general activity of exchange. A one-sided, imperfect, and therefore unfair exchange can be described by the term "karmic burden." This sets a mechanism for the balance of energetic relationships into motion. The more and the longer the participating parties maintain an imbalance, the more vehement its effect will be. This ensures that the "spoilsports" will be limited in their capacity to act or that they are "thrown off" the playing field so they don't stand around like an obstacle and take the space away from others who also would like to participate. Be aware of the far-reaching consequences of this law for longevity, healing, and success. A comprehensive work could be written about just the implications of this rule.

The second law says that nothing has an exact double in its essential energy pattern in this world. This means that each being is unique and has unmatched talents. As a result, every living being is important and indispensable for evolution on a fundamental level. Who or what could otherwise replace its special contribution? We should be aware of the consequences that this law has for our self-image and our concepts of other beings' value!

The third law says all substances and energies that are absorbed, transformed, and eliminated by a being are inseparably impregnated with its essential energy pattern through this process. This means that everything we absorb and truly utilize within ourselves will carry the stamp of our individuality with it out into the world to be spread. None of our uniqueness ever really gets lost!

The fourth law says that, no matter on what level, everything that we take in and include in our metabolism gives us the possibility of absorbing the individual imprint that it contains as information into our system, without erasing it in the process. This means that we can almost* grow automatically if we just participate in the exchange processes of the universe that come to us.

The fifth law says that the respective pattern of one being contains information on various levels and that the more material and tangible such information is, the more unconsciously and automatically it can be integrated into our system. So we hardly need to pay attention to our material metabolism. We eat and breathe, and our body does the rest while we concern ourselves with other things. The subtler the information is, the more aware we must be in order to integrate it into our system. This means, for example, that we don't necessarily have to become conscious on the purely physical level for healing and development to occur. But on the spiritual,

---

* The "almost" is explained by the next law.

subtle levels, healing and development aren't possible without the expansion of consciousness. And, as a further conclusion: the more consciously we deal with the world, the greater our spiritual development will be.

The sixth law says that every conscious exchange process, which touches all the levels to the same extent and takes place without reservations, creates a direct connection to the level of unity for the affected being. We could also call this the state of enlightenment because the yin energy, as an expression and the essence of earthly Creation (the material form), is connected without any inhibitions and hesitations through this unconditional creative and loving act to the yang energy (an expression of heaven and its essence). The switch is turned on, the energy can flow, and the lamp shines, enlightenment has taken place!

In order to let this type of absolute exchange behavior occur, some practice is necessary. We must create a lack of intention so that nothing more blocks the flow of the forces. This functions only when we have understood that everything coming to us is absolutely valuable, important, unique, and exactly appropriate for us in particular because the universe doesn't make any inappropriate offers. This eliminates the fear of not getting something that we believe we absolutely need. Enlightened people don't have an apathetic attitude based on disinterest. On the contrary, they are extremely interested in the things that come to them. Because of their wisdom, they have truly understood and accepted the meaning of these things. This is why they accept them without hesitation and deliberation. Enlightenment is therefore the result of proper participation in the processes of exchange.

The seventh law says that every being can determine the speed of information absorption and integration on its own, thereby determining its own growth on all levels in a completely free manner. It does this by a) directing its consciousness only to certain levels and focusing on the promotion of its development there and b) by absorbing the information carriers from the constantly ample offering that can most easily be used and utilized in its current condition. In the practice, this means that the more you know our own strengths and weaknesses, the easier and more quickly we can progress on our path. Here as well, the degree of our consciousness is ultimately the deciding factor.

Exchange and the Seven Major Chakras

Now let's take a brief look at the seven levels upon which the energy exchange takes place before we examine the practical application of this profound knowledge in our everyday lives.

On the first level, our root chakra is affected. An exchange here should ensure and strengthen our ability to survive in the broadest sense of the word.

On the second level, our love-of-life and relationships chakra is affected. An exchange here should ensure and strengthen our ability to have relationships in the broadest sense, as well as creating joy and a feeling of harmonious fulfillment.

On the third level, our power, analysis, and digestion chakra is affected. An exchange here should analyze our personal ability to be powerful, to ensure and strengthen our possibilities on all levels of existence, and to digest materials and energies.

On the fourth level, our heart chakra is affected. An exchange here should ensure and strengthen our ability to love, synthesize, and integrate.

On the fifth level, our throat chakra is affected. An exchange here should ensure and strengthen our ability of self-expression, communication, self-experience, and self-fulfillment in all areas of our being.

On the sixth level, our forehead chakra, our third eye, is affected. An exchange here should ensure and strengthen our ability to perceive and find our path in the broadest sense of the word.

On the seventh level, our crown chakra is affected. An exchange here should ensure and strengthen our ability to experience God in everything that exists. However, once we have accepted the lower six levels with all of their possibilities, the seventh will automatically be included.

There naturally is still a great deal to be said about the various meanings of the seven levels or seven chakras. Further information can be found in the Appendix 2 and the Commented Bibliography contains interesting standard works on this topic. In any case, it is useful to become fundamentally acquainted with these correlations. In all types of exchange processes, we can attempt to understand which of the elements described here are particularly emphasized by our exchange partners and whether they actually appeal to them. Next, we can focus on ourselves to see which levels within us have the greatest need for exchange at the moment. Then we can decide whether or not our needs are being adequately considered in the trade. Here's an example of this: When a man needs new tires for his car and spontaneously decides upon a certain brand that is depicted in the familiar advertising with an appealing woman, he would basically probably like to have a girlfriend, which is suggestively associated with the brand through the advertising. If it becomes clear to him that his unsatisfied needs are leading him up the garden path, he can learn to look for a partner and the right tires—but separately—and therefore with the prospects of true success and actual satisfaction of his desires!

Five Rules for Enlightenment through a Harmonious Exchange in Everyday Life

How can these perceptions be integrated into our everyday lives? There is a simple way of doing this—namely, the path of least resistance. Every time that we get into an exchange situation, we can act according to the following, five-step plan:

1. Accept joy

If we are happy with what is offered on an emotional level and it (adequately) satisfies our true needs (these two points are often the most important), as well as appearing to be worth the price to be paid after we have thoroughly considered it, then we can accept it and enjoy being permitted to own and use it.

2. Avoid difficulties

If what is offered can't (adequately) fulfill our true desires or if it doesn't appear to be worth the price and we still have the choice, then we can leave it alone and look for something else that may appeal much more to us.

3. Adapt what doesn't fit

If what is offered doesn't quite work out for us, but we must accept it for some reason, then we can use all our means to try to understand its benefit. We can use it in a way that gives us a great deal of joy and satisfaction. In most cases, we can usually change and understand something to the point that even if we didn't want it at first, it becomes something that we learn to value and have fun with.

4. Learn patience

If we don't like what has been offered to us, but must accept it for some reason, and can neither make it suitable nor understand and transform its meaning for ourselves, then we can practice being patient. At the very least, patience is a quality we can always learn, as well as being a valuable treasure. Then we can attempt to somehow accept the exchanged possession without constantly being dissatisfied or annoyed as a result. It is difficult enough to have to deal with something we don't like. So we shouldn't make things even harder for ourselves by continually producing stress that we could actually avoid!

5. Develop new ways of thinking

As an expansion of the last step, so that we can still make something out of our supposedly useless new possession: completely change our attitude toward this article. We can look at it from a totally different perspective. Ask other people how they would meaningfully put it to use, read books about it, collect information from other perspectives that could still help us achieve a sensible and beneficial use of our property. We might even try working with oracles. But we should keep trying until we've found a solution. This always works and will give us the most satisfaction. It opens up completely new opportunities of growth and will ultimately be the most fun for us. The precondition for this is for that we must be stubborn.* And don't give up until we succeed!

If we take these principles to heart and also translate them into action, we are certain to become enlightened. Particularly in business life, we can achieve a great deal of success and simultaneously develop our personality by using the laws and tips in this chapter. For example: We can take one whole day to apply the principles presented here by writing down the solution possibilities for our occupational problems. Another approach is to also use the pendulum tables in Appendix 1 and the "Chakra-Oriented Oracle" in Appendix 2 for this purpose. However, even just the suggestions in this chapter can show us the way to enjoyment and success!

---

* Also see: Step 4 (Learn patience)

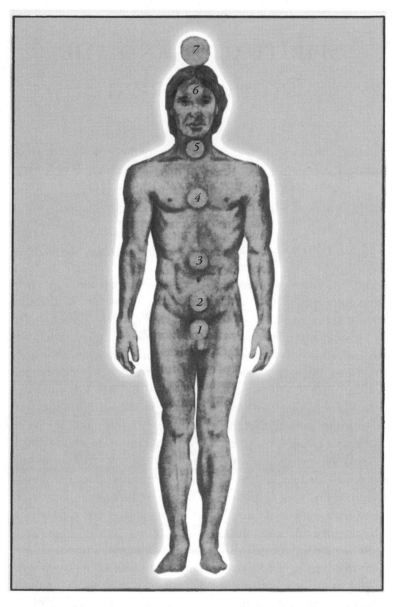

The seven major energy centers (chakras) of a human being

1. Base of Spine Center, 2. Lower Abdom Center, 3. Solar Plexus Center,
4. Heart Center, 5. Throat Center, 6. Forehead Center,
7. Crown Chakra

Chapter 7

SPIRITUALITY AND THE STOCK MARKET

Why am I discussing such an apparently profane topic like the stock market in connection with spirituality? I hope you will be lenient with me and continue reading for the time being.

An I Ching Apprentice on the Stock Market

In my "wild years" as a speculator in stocks and securities, I naturally tested every esoteric tool with which I was familiar for its suitability in the practice and hard reality of the stock market. This included the I Ching, an ancient and very comprehensive Chinese oracle system, which has now become my constant companion and absolutely trustworthy adviser. As I worked on a great variety of stock-market problems with it, which could ultimately be summarized by the sentence: "How do I get as much money as possible as quickly as possible," I soon noticed that the I Ching was actually working on me. Like a wise teacher, it helped me with certain speculations, but it also told me very clearly when I had overdone my greed for money and actually would be better off attending to my personal growth instead of my bank account. No matter what tricks and strategies I then tried in order to keep asserting my will, it saw through me and remained uncompromising.

At some point I finally understood and accepted that there was more involved here. I asked what I should actually do with the I Ching at the stock market. Surprisingly, it told me that I could learn to understand the principles of cosmic order, the law of yin and yang, as well as the perpetual problems of people, their fear and greed, in a comprehensive and practice-oriented manner. So the I Ching helped me to comprehend the ups and downs of the securities prices and goods prices as an earthly correlation to the cosmic flow of energy. I learned to interpret the behavior of the stock-exchange operators as an expression of typically human qualities that I also encountered time and again in everyday life, in other professions, and in the esoteric scene. The ancient oracle showed me how our approach to money, occupation, and possessions is a precise reflection of our ability to love, our fears, and the development of our spirituality. In the process, I lost many illusions about myself. As a result, I learned to better understand the world and my own being.

This process also led me to teachers like Andre Kostolany, a Grand Old Man of the stock market who, with his humanity and naturalness, was an important role model for me over a long period of time. Kostolany approaches material matters from a perspective influenced by philosophy and musicality that causes the hair of "financial technicians" to stand on end—and he is successful with it! Adopting his stock-market philosophy planted the seeds through which my human aptitudes could develop and my financial investments could grow.

When I overcome difficulties in my life today or help others find and apply meaningful solutions to their problems in a holistic sense, I draw on this wisdom and the experiences that my "Chinese master" directly or indirectly gave me through human mediators. Now I would like to share some of this wealth and show how people, no matter whether they are concerned with securities speculation and financial transactions or with esotericism and spirituality, repeatedly display the same behavior and the same motives. By observing the behavior of people who are concerned with material values, we can develop a profound, spiritual understanding of the world. And, what is most important about this type of learning is that it isn't academic, unrealistic, and unsuited for everyday life. Instead, it is a type of learning that draws from "normal" life to make it possible for us to live every day in a spiritual way that creates happiness.

The times in which people interested in esotericism went out into the wilderness to be hermits in order to find fulfillment are finally over at the beginning of the Age of Aquarius. Today, it's important to put the life of each individual into a spiritual context, once again letting the vibration of light and love become a part of our world. This is certainly a tremendous challenge for all of us, yet an even greater opportunity. There are enough problems that have remained unsolved for too long and too many people who suffer and are hopeless. We can't afford to keep trying to assert our wills instead of recognizing the universal laws of life on earth.

If we finally decide to perceive and use the esoteric aspect of money, industry, technology, and science, a golden age will be waiting for us. We need to look at what there is to learn and use it to bring love into our lives and our surrounding environment.

The Tough Guys and the Soft Guys

An important factor for increasing or falling prices on the stock market is the psychological situation of the market participants. Andre Kostolany taught me to understand and value the difference between "tough" and "soft" investors. This rough, yet profound characterization can be successfully applied to much more than just the financial markets. It also applies to every other area of human life. Why should a fundamental pattern of the personality just be effective in one direction? It is particularly interesting to illuminate the two behavior structures in the area of esotericism and self-realization. This makes it easier to understand many of the strange figures in the "esoteric scene." As a result of this understanding, we can help ourselves and others approach the processes of self-realization in a more meaningful manner and avoid dead-end streets. And should our path include the private or professional pre-occupation with money, we will also be able to use this knowledge with much success in this area since these laws are universally valid.

Two types of human beings, the tough guys and the soft guys, largely determine the stock-market courses. According to whether more of the one camp or the other is active in the securities markets, the chances are greater that the prices will rise or fall. If there are primarily tough guys on the market, the prices of selected solid stocks will rise slowly or stay just about the same with a relatively small turnover. Even if there is bad news from the economy or politics, the prices still won't give way in a disproportionate manner, and the mood still remains relatively relaxed.

If there are more soft guys in the market, there is a tendency to be more hectic. The prices of many stocks will climb quickly with large turnovers until the prices are hopelessly exorbitant. Then they fall in great leaps and with a hysterical atmosphere. When there is good or bad news, the market reacts with a disproportionately strong range of price movements, whereby the news is frequently evaluated in a completely illogical way. Why this process repeatedly takes place in the same manner can be explained through the totally different behavior of both groups of market participants.

The Behavior of the Tough Guys

Here's an exact description of how the so-called tough guys behave: They carefully and patiently collect information about the market situation, the peripheral economic conditions, the psychological makeup of the market participants, and the state of specific stock corporations. They attentively listen to the assessments of other people who have comprehensible explanations of the current situation and have a good reputation in their business practices. This is how they get ideas for their own evaluation of the circumstances. But in no case would they simply assume someone else's standpoint or strategy of action. Instead, they ultimately always take care of their own business themselves and like to make the effort to think about things and struggle to form their own opinion. They know that it is this exact exertion that brings lasting success with it.

They don't take it seriously when people promise them mountains of gold on the basis of windy, less realistic theories or want to takes money out of their pockets by talking about catastrophes such as inflation, war, conspiracies, and bank collapses. They may waste some time with them just as a break from their daily business, but only to amuse themselves.

Once they have formed a well-founded opinion, they take money that they aren't dependent on, still keeping some in reserve so that they can make use of more favorable prices—and invest it according to their perspectives. It remains in these investments, even if the stock prices should suddenly drop for a while, until there is a lasting change of the overall situation that makes a sale appear to really be meaningful. The tough guys get in on certain securities when the majority of the stock-market participants is pessimistic and sells off its stocks at the lowest prices; they sell them when the majority of the market participants (again, the soft guys) are euphoric and, because of a belief in the continually rising price, get in at almost any price.

The behavior of the tough guys is called "anti-cyclical," and this is how a lot of money can be earned in a calm manner. The behavior of the soft guys can be termed "cyclical," and, in most cases, this is how people can lose money and the health of their nerves. The tough guys don't look at the prices of their stocks every day because they have planned for long-term success. Instead, they attentively observe whether there have been changes in the important data of the economy or the enterprises in which they are interested. They know that the prices are the long-term result of these changes and short-term swings are insignificant. This is why they can sleep peacefully and be relaxed about their daily business, using the money they have earned to give more quality to their lives and those of their fellow human beings.

We can have wonderful conversations about art, culture, and philosophy with "tough" stock-market operators. It's easy to party and be happy with them. They are open to the beautiful things of life and want to enjoy their existence. At peace with themselves, they trust in their abilities and luck without giving in to greed as a result. They don't get involved in speculations that would exceed their limitations, which they know very well. In this way, they don't become involved in existence-threatening situations that would intensify their fears so much that they could no longer think clearly. This is why they aren't slaves to their material goods.

The Behavior of the Soft Guys

In somewhat generalized terms, the soft guys have a completely different approach. For example, they frantically collect information from the media, which has a very sensationalist orientation, or listen spellbound to the "experts" who scream the loudest and tell of the enormous fortunes that they have created for their clients. The soft guys then like to buy whatever has been recommended in this manner. These recommendations are usually the same things with which umpteen generations of soft guys have been deceived: options, dead-end stocks from far away countries (the further, the better), distant enterprises, or from exotic lines of business about which there is very little concrete information but abundant rumors of trailblazing inventions or hidden treasures. These naturally include gold in every form, real estate in distant lands, accounts and insurance in tax-exempt nations. They are also influenced by books, magazines, and seminars on these topics.

The soft guys also like to orient themselves toward people who claim that they are among the few with a grasp of the situation and have therefore recognized the coming catastrophes in time. Of course, the soft guys then want to buy what these "catastrophe gurus" recommend to them—and also sell to them—as a means of survival. These are usually the same things: gold, real estate (in "safe" countries), insurance, books, magazines, and seminars (in which there are also reports about catastrophes), or stocks from exotic companies that will supposedly profit from the coming end of the world.

If someone claims that he is being persecuted, repressed, and forced to be silent by the media, politicians, or established experts because they are afraid that his competence or the dissemination of his information might harm their dark goals if the public knew about them, he is immediately well-accepted by the soft guys. With joyful and sympathetic hearts, they will buy what he recommends. And they will slap each other on the shoulders and feel that they are in good hands in a community of conspirators composed of a few informed people who will manage to cope because of their trust in the right thing. But instead, they naturally find themselves in the not-so-small circle of the eternally deceived. If well-meaning tough guys try to discuss their convictions with them and get them to think about things, the soft guys feel their suspicions totally confirmed. Their advisers had already told them that, if they want to cope with things, they must be trusting and not succumb to the insinuations of others who are wrongly informed.

Both the catastrophe scenario and the "I'm the person who can make you tremendously rich" sales strategies have the most success when the economy is running well and also when it functions quite poorly. In extreme situations, people's fears and greed can be appealed to most easily. Particularly in these times, many people are looking for a leader who promises to give them what they want to have, but believe they aren't capable of achieving on their own because of lacking self-trust. So a strong leader must be found. Many soft guys also like to orient themselves toward what "everyone says." If the stock-market prices are low and pessimism reigns in the media, they will sell their securities because they believe it can only get worse from now on and, in any case, society is at an end.

The tough guys then like to buy the stocks that the soft guys are selling dirt cheap because they know that every low is followed by a high*, and that the more people believe things are going down the drain, the more quickly the prices will rise. If the prices do subsequently increase, the soft guys stay pessimistic at first and comfort themselves with the thought that this improvement is just a last flickering of the extinguishing fire of the economy, after which things will definitely and inevitably fall into ruin. As prices continue to rise, they become insecure and then only buy hesitantly; but soon, more hectically as prices rise, and often they are even seduced by their greed to buy on credit because now "everyone" is saying that things are really improving and it can only get better. Now they are convinced that they have finally received the best deal.

They naturally get their stocks from the tough guys who, in a time of upward exaggeration, are once again acting in an anti-cyclical manner and selling their stocks in order to rake in the terrific profits that they have been able to amass in the meantime. If the stock prices fall once again in keeping with the law of yin and yang, the tough guys have feathered their own nests.

The soft guys initially comfort themselves with the thought that the fall in prices is only a temporary weakness and the promised enormous rise will now finally come. As a result, they continue to

---

By the way, this is a consistent interpretation regarding the principle of the eternal interplay between the cosmic forces handed down since ancient times in the Taoist yin/yang monad (see illustration). The stronger an energy quality is, the greater the probability that it will evoke its opposite.

The role of the media in this process is quite interesting. Contrary to common opinion, the media hardly ever creates trends but only intensifies those that already exist because they are listening to the people and reacting to their wishes and longings; the more superficially they do this, the more successful they are at it.

buy the stocks that have now become much too expensive from their advisors, who now want to get rid of them for a good reason. The prices naturally continue to fall and many soft guys are now forced to sell their stocks at bad prices since their banks want to have the loans back. Now that the stocks serving as security for the borrowed money have an increasingly lower value with the falling prices, the credit institutions are understandably worried and want to correct the situation before their debtors become unable to pay.

In this manner, many soft guys lose their money and (once again) feel cheated by the evil stock market. Very few seek the blame for this disaster where it actually lies: in their own weaknesses. Yet, there are still some for whom such an experience is a healing shock. They start out on the difficult, but proper path of self-perception and attempt to work on themselves in order to avoid future errors instead of blaming others for their problems or expecting others to think for them.

The Taoist yin/yang monad

Every Tough Guy Was Once a Soft Guy

Now please don't think that people come into the world sorted into two groups of "soft" and "tough." Every human being first starts out as a soft guy since we are all sent into the world in this initial state so we can grow and learn through our mistakes—and, this is the most important point, to have the opportunity of knowing and learning to love what is weak and eternally imperfect within us and other people. If we were all perfect, we would never have the opportunity of developing unconditional love, the most important ability of all.

Fear, Greed, and Enlightenment

In the course of our lives we are confronted with our fears or our greed. This ultimately leads us to an attempt to create the most complete security possible and thereby suppress our fears. The result is the opportunity for learning. Whenever we let our thoughts and actions become determined by fear or greed, we will fail. In order to understand this, it is necessary to precisely understand the roles of fear and greed in human life, as well as the areas where they shouldn't exert such an influence. Experiences of enlightenment automatically result when a person has learned to live on the basis of love and understanding instead of fear and greed.

What is the Purpose of Fear?

Fear is fundamentally a very important and useful function. It can be defined as a mechanism that constantly directs all the sensory perceptions to look for indications of situations in which the respective person has already been and has experienced as oppressive, creating suffering, and/or causing pain. If a corresponding pattern is noticed, a more or less intense feeling of unease is produced according to the degree of presumed danger. In the extreme case, this can escalate into panic so that the potential danger is communicated to the conscious mind. This causes it to react in a way that either reduces or eliminates the danger. The pattern of these fear-causing relationships is stored in the subconscious mind of every human being and is constantly available. It means an important opportunity for automatically recognizing familiar dangers and difficulties and avoiding them in due time in order to make life easier. Whether or not we flee, when and how we do flee, get help, or deal with the situation in some other way that reduces the problem, is largely regulated to bypass the conscious mind so that the reactions take place as swiftly as possible. The more quickly we react in a fear situation, the longer we will normally survive. So fear is a useful survival mechanism in and of itself.

The Dangers of the Fear Automatism

The catch in the whole matter is that the patterns of fear-recognition and the reaction to fear have always been formed in the past. Consequently, they take into consideration the abilities and shortcomings existing at points in time occurring more or less in the distant past. In the extreme case, these patterns are based on the possible reactions of a small child. When a child who is imprinted in this manner matures and doesn't create any possibilities for itself to become attuned to its growing opportunities and the changed situation, the meaningful automatisms will become increasingly absurd during the course of time. These will eventually become completely outdated and, through their intervention in many situations, reduce the person who now is actually an adult to one having the abilities of a small child. A comparison between a frequently occurring small child's fear-recognition/reaction pattern and the corresponding adult reality should make this situation more evident.

When we are confronted with a situation that we can't assess because of our lack of experience and knowledge, the fear mechanism evaluates it as being threatening. Small children react in the following manner: Running away and hiding (attitude of denial) or fleeing to father or mother (in the case of a "childish" adult, to an authority figure who corresponds with the image of the inner father or the inner mother) and seeking protection. They trust that this person at its side will be able to master the difficulties with his or her own possibilities, which appear unbelievably large to children.

Adults react like this: Through precise observation and becoming involved in the unfamiliar circumstances in a controlled way that takes their known possibilities into account. They collects additional information, as well as hearing the advice of people who are or have been in similar situations, exchanging opinions and ideas with them, and getting information from other sources. In the process, all the new information is examined to see whether it appears comprehensible and sensible. The knowledge that can't be questioned even after careful examination is accepted and tried out in practice to determine whether it can be meaningfully used with the available opportunities. This is how adults who act on the basis of their own responsibility (I could also say "tough guys" here) expands their opportunities step-by-step in a controlled exchange with the surrounding world until these are adequate for evaluating and mastering the problem situation. Through the intensive process of being involved with the new situation, the fear-recognition and reaction patterns are also brought up-to-date. These patterns have time to grow and open up for changes through the conscious approach to the situation.

In the first case, the responsibility for one's own well-being is assigned to another person, without using the opportunity for learning and growth. In the second case, every opportunity of development is seized and personal security is preserved at the same time. Each of us is forced to begin our path in life with the first pattern, but isn't it much more satisfying and useful to follow the second possibility as an adult? A closer look at the issue of greed is certain to make the choice even easier.

What is the Meaning of Greed?

Greed can be defined as a boundless and thoughtless grasping and exploiting of a situation as the opportunity for satisfying our needs. The intense damage to our environment through the exploitation of its resources is an example of greedy behavior. How does this type of behavior come about?

Greed is excessive desire, a desire of which we are almost at the mercy without any defenses because of its intensity. Whenever people don't have the opportunity of adequately satisfying their fundamental needs, a sense of security, love, affirmation of the self, relationships, affection, and physical desire, intense fear-recognition and re-action patterns (see above) are activated. The fulfillment of these needs is absolutely necessary over the long term for the mental, emotional, and physical health of a human being. These patterns always trigger a stronger desire for the satisfaction of needs, which becomes increasingly less differentiated through the course of time.

Here is an example: a man doesn't get enough affection from his partner. At first, he will keep attempting to somehow get his companion's loving attention by enticing her, fighting with her, or trying to blackmail her. If this doesn't work, he might perhaps try his luck with other partners who seem to be suitable to him. If this attempt is also unsuccessful, his selection criterion for potential partners becomes defined in increasingly broader terms. If this also doesn't satisfy his needs or if this solution isn't acceptable, the need is frequently shifted to other areas and he seeks the fulfillment of his desires in an addiction.* In keeping with his personal preferences and prejudices, he will use alcohol, food, smoking, work, buying things that are somehow related to the fulfillment of his desires, the pursuit of money and possessions, or an intensive occupation with hobbies of all types to reduce this deficit. These are naturally all just insufficient substitute gratifications, through which the actual hunger only becomes weaker for a short period of time, becoming all the more intense again afterward.

The following chart, clearly portrays a graphic picture of these correlations. This incomplete satisfaction in particular produces the vicious circle. Immediately after the substitutive gratification has been experienced, a certain satisfaction is perceptible. But this quickly passes because the stimulation has just covered superficial portions of the deep desires. The simplest way to again obtain the desired feeling is to experience the substitute gratification once more. This person, who is basically sensible, is now chasing after money, cigarettes, sex, work, or possessions as if their life depended upon it.

---

* Unfulfilled basic needs are responsible for the creation of all types of addictions.

And this is also basically true since their essential needs are at least being satisfied a little. In order to no longer feel the pain of rejection, he has long forgotten or suppressed that there are also better possibilities of getting what he needs. So he desperately clings to the vicious circle—until he becomes ill because of exhaustion or is so battered by fate (for example: losing money on the stock market) that he attempts to direct his life into a different, healthier course.

How the Craving for Substitutional Gratification Arises from Unsatisfied Basic Needs

Levels upon which the basic needs can be satisfied in a way that is least natural and also least lasting, in which the goal or the surrounding environment no longer corresponds with the actual desire.

Shifting of longing for fulfillment of needs to other goals that are relatively easy to attain and experienced as connected to the actual goal.

Concentration on fulfillment of needs, whereby the type of surrounding environment becomes increasingly insignificant. (Shift of surrounding environment)

Search for a more favorable surrounding environment with decreasing orientation toward the familiar surrounding environment. (Shift of surrounding environment)

Fight to fulfill needs in the familiar surrounding environment. (Recognition of deficit)

Levels upon which the basic needs can be satisfied most naturally and lastingly.

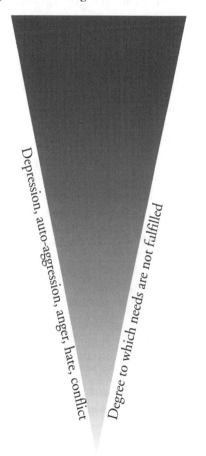

Depression, auto-aggression, anger, hate, conflict

Degree to which needs are not fulfilled

Basic emotional needs:
Physical desire, affirmation of self, affection, relationships, love

Fear as a Survival Mechanism

Fear can therefore be summarized as an important survival mechanism that functions meaningfully as long as a person deals with the demands of life in a conscious and responsible manner. Unconsciously approaching problems and shifting the responsibility for directly coping with difficulties to others* does not give the fear automatism adequate opportunities. It needs these opportunities so that it can adapt to an expansion of personal abilities or changes in the surrounding environment. This results in a permanent situation of fear since the person perceives, at least on the subconscious level, a dependency upon others for the maintenance of life and satisfaction of needs. At the same time, this weakens the sense of self-assurance. When a person is motivated in this way, it becomes obvious that there is a temptation to subliminally manipulate others so that they are always within reach and on call when needed to fulfill one's own wishes. These people will simultaneously take advantage of as many opportunities to satisfy needs as possible (eating, drinking, smoking, working, speculating in the stock market, etc.).

Greed is the result since new satisfaction must constantly be sought, but ultimately only gives short-term fulfillment: It doesn't reach the true goals of the longings. Since this surrogate usually isn't available quickly enough, in an adequate amount, and at any time, the wish to gather "provisions" arises in order to avoid the painful situation of once again not having one's needs met. This is a constant state of stress that ties up increasingly more time and energy the longer it lasts. If we ask one of these desperate, struggling people why they don't use the objects of value that they have stockpiled in order to enjoy, the response will probably be that then they soon wouldn't have anything left and would wind up on the street. The primitive fear of being defenseless and helplessly at the mercy of a hostile surrounding world is seething deep within them.

---

* Many parents promote this behavior by attempting to assume as much responsibility as possible on behalf of their children. This naturally imprints this pattern deeply in a person's character and even leads to the grown-up child still being inclined to hand over responsibility to others.

This complex pattern forms the foundation for the behavior of the soft guys mentioned above. This kind of constant, grim battling for a little bit of happiness in life can also be found in the esoteric scene

Chasing Enlightenment

Enlightenment—Many people seek it and do almost anything for it, or at least for the people who they think could provide them with it. True to the pattern described above, they look for the "right" guru, the "right" exercise, the "right" book, and the "latest" liberating perception. But in the maze of the many seminars, teachers, and paths, hardly anyone finds what he or she truly longs for. This in no way implies that the teachers, books, and paths have no meaningful messages to offer. The problem is just that the messenger is usually considered more important than the message. If there is a wonderful energy experience, a spontaneous healing, or the perception of the presence of God close to a teacher, many people react by continuing to seek contact with the mediator of the experience instead of the experience itself. In the wink of an eye, a pedestal is built and the chosen guru placed upon it, whether he wants this or not. Instead of pursuing the question as to what could be done to produce this same type of experience, this task is now assigned to the mediator. Many little children in the costumes of adults then dance around him and applaud him.

In any case, this lasts as long as he shows them the qualities of parental omnipotence that they wish from him. If he becomes too human, their interest in him extinguishes or changes into rejection since the person who is evil in their eyes has disappointed them and not kept the promises that they had hoped from him. So he isn't omnipotent after all and therefore unacceptable as a teacher. So, on to the next guru! Perhaps the next person will be better at playing the game of "be my big mommy/daddy!"

Many Paths to the Same Goal

Esotericists seek enlightenment and stock-market speculators seek wealth. Both of these states can never really be achieved through another person taking our place on the path meant for us, but through our own accomplishment and experience. Both groups ultimately seek absolute security and the guarantee of happiness and success. However, no one can ever find this security in the outside world. No one can take on the risk of life for another person.

Stock Market and Esoteric Scene: Gurus Here and Gurus There

In both areas, on the stock market and in the esoteric scene, there are various types of teachers. The more they acknowledge their fallibility and vulnerability, the better and more honest they are. Only through these qualities can they experience their mistakes and learn a great deal from them in order to further develop themselves. As a result, they can especially love themselves and others because of their weaknesses, including them in their thoughts and actions. This may make sense in the spiritual realm—but why should this also apply to the stock market?

The answer is quite simple—the greatest obstacles in the path to becoming a successful stock-market speculator in the long-term are fear, greed, and a lack of consciousness. Only those who can deal with their own feelings without suppressing them, but also without being at their mercy and losing the big picture, can make sensible decisions. In the long run, only those who invest using their common sense can keep their money and have good chances of multiplying it. The conscious approach to experiences in the here and now is an indispensable precondition for perceiving changes in the economic and political situation.

Those who are too fixated upon tomorrow and the day-after-tomorrow or yesterday and the day-before-yesterday will overlook the opportunities that they can only use today. "Consciousness, you monks, is everything!" This wise old Zen saying not only applies to the path of enlightenment, but also to the everyday life of a stock-market speculator.

Stock-market gurus who can even laugh about themselves and not take their theories too seriously have enough distance to open up to the constantly changing situations in the markets. Because they know themselves, perceive their own weaknesses and strengths and include these in their own considerations, they are successful. Only those who know themselves can know God! Students of any path can orient themselves to their living example and the experience that they have dealt with in order to stay on the path to light and/or success and not stumble on difficult terrain. But each of them must walk the path alone. Always! If we have truly understood and accepted this, then we are already close—to wealth or enlightenment, according to what we want. But if we have truly walked this and become a "tough guy" in the process, when we reach the goal we will recognize that the fulfillment of *all* true wishes occurs there. As different as life may be, if we discover its esoteric, meaning hidden, side, everything we do will be spiritual, filled with the divine spirit. And there isn't anything more that can be attained in this world. Once we are there, we won't even want anything more.

The Dabbler Market and Small-Time Esotericism

Back to the stock market: When the prices rise for a longer period of time, increasingly more soft guys have the courage to invest in all types of securities. They quickly equip themselves with some type of pseudo-wisdom about the economy and finance markets. Then they know by heart the most wide-spread prejudices and phrases in this genre, which they find so fascinating. They like to repeat these platitudes frequently in conversations with like-minded people, without having a true basic understanding of anything they are saying. To someone new on the stock market, such a half-educated soft guy appears to be a demigod: "All the people and things he knows! And much of what he tells so easily is also written in the newspaper! He must be an initiate!"

So it happens that even people who hardly have the faintest idea about the world of the stock market and economics suddenly feel themselves to be competent experts. They are even treated as such by people who know even less but are impressed by boastful behavior. We could call this constellation of public psychology the dabbler market. (Webster's definition of "dabble": to work at anything in an irregular or superficial manner.)

When the general euphoria about rising prices causes many dabblers to buy stocks or snap up a few stock-market phrases in order to put in a word, it's high time for the tough guys to get out. This is because an uncomprehending investment public drives the prices in directions that aren't predictable since they follow no logic.

The urge to buy or sell is primarily motivated by feelings like fear and greed (see above), and fear will always ultimately assert itself. This means panic buying, which creates a strong bear* market. In this type of dabbler market, fan clubs are quickly formed on both a small and large scale. Some pseudo-competent soft guys have quite a distinct talent for advertising and can sell themselves well. They hold seminars, write books, publish stock-market letters, and found financial consulting firms. A bull** market sometimes lasts for several years and their business runs well during this time. Many of these people truly believe what they tell their customers; when a bear market comes, they are totally perplexed and no longer understand the world.

In the esoteric scene, it isn't unusual for similar situations to occur. Wherever people are concerned with self-realization and spiritual paths, we will meet individuals who act very serious, holy, and important; they constantly talk about seminars, books, spiritual teachers, channeling, reincarnation, meditation, and anything else that happens to be currently in fashion in the scene. Phrases like "that's karmic" and "I feel so close to you and somehow sense that we were together in an earlier life!" are offered in constantly changing variations and rated as a sign of "high spirituality." We could call this manifestation of the self-realization scene "small-time esotericism."

---

* Bear market: stock-market jargon for a time in which the prices are falling on a wide front.
** Bull market: stock-market jargon for a time in which the prices are rising on a wide front.

As in the dabbler market, fears and greed essentially motivate people who behave in this manner. This is why they are also practically magically attracted to topics like "immortality for everyone through a few simple physical exercises/nutritional guidelines," "wealth through positive thinking," "always doing the right thing with the channeled advice of high spiritual beings," or "how I can influence others so they do what I want them to do" and "how can I rescue myself from the threatening end of the world."

Magic is the general term for these related topics. In recent years, the occupation with esoteric wisdom has experienced a tremendous boom in the Western world. Many "old hats" have been dyed a different color and given new names. Most people who engage in esoteric exercises and theories in a practical sense look down upon becoming involved with magic. This sounds like evil and the work of the Devil, and we all want to live in love and light. However, this is really just the surface since the areas in which all types of magicians have been involved since ancient times (and this can be historically proved beyond a shadow of a doubt) are the following: immortality, wealth, communication with spirit beings to obtain important information, influencing other people according to one's own ideas, and protection from threatening catastrophes. All of this is interesting knowledge for people who are horribly afraid of aging, death, and helplessness; who are afraid of not receiving enough to fulfill their needs; who are afraid of not having enough self-confidence in terms of making the right decision; who prefer to subliminally manipulate others instead of taking the risk of saying what they want and confronting other people on a level of equality.

As applies to other goods as well, the label doesn't always describe the actual contents. The use of the words love, God, and light may possibly just be a cheap whitewash to hide the fears behind them. There is basically nothing objectionable about magic, as long as this tool kit is used in a responsible, and therefore honest, manner.

But when people talk about it being an act of love when we, supported by a breathing method, pray to the angels or Jesus so that they give us a free parking spot or money for our vacation, the whole matter becomes quite questionable. When we receive something that we have requested in such a magical manner*, then someone else must give it up. If this other person doesn't receive a fair exchange from us, a karmic debt will be created. This is a relationship that hasn't been completed harmoniously in the cosmic sense. The more things are amassed in this manner, the more intense the energetic pressure attempting to create a balance will become. According to the motto of: "And if you are not willing, I will force you!" the debt is forcibly collected at some point since the universe could otherwise suffer damage to its structure.

For all that, there are still many people who make the effort to deal with their spiritual development in a wide-awake and responsible manner.

Synthesis: Turning Our Mistakes into the Engine of Our Success

In this chapter, I have depicted how the tough guys and the soft guys behave in quite a drastic manner at times to clearly present the issues. However, in practice there is no clear separation between black and white, good and evil, naive and comprehending. The shades of gray dominate! We all have the tough guy and the soft guy within us. This is also good since it keeps us awake and willing to learn.

No matter what we've learned and how far we've come – we will always make mistakes because of the soft guy within us—and then continue learning because of the mistakes! That's what they are there for. Thank God that they are as indelible as our talents. Together, both maintain the natural harmony within us. Strengths and weaknesses are yang and yin. We can learn from our weaknesses in order to continue developing our strengths. We can learn to live with our weaknesses and lovingly accept the soft guy within us. We can learn to laugh at ourselves and experience how wealthy and enlightened this makes us when we don't take enlightenment and wealth all that seriously. We only receive what we strive for when we let go of it. Is this a paradox? Perhaps, but it's true. As long as we want something, we are tense and concentrated. Enlightenment can only take

---

* The use of holy names doesn't preclude the use of magic. Magic essentially means that someone wants to obtain irresistible means of power.

place when we no longer make our own will paramount but the quality that is the essence of God: unconditional love.

The same also applies to wealth. Who has more? Is it a person who works around the clock for $1,000,000 a month or the individual who obtains all the experiences of learning and happiness he needs in order to feel good, to grow, and be healthy for $1,000 a month?

To Clear Away Any Misunderstandings...

In case you now think that earning a lot of money would be an obstacle on your path to yourself, then read the first three chapters of this book. Neither too much money nor too little money is the key to happiness and a fulfilled life. It always depends on what you do with it...

The Universal Laws of Success for the Stock Market and for Spiritual Development

At the conclusion of this chapter, there are a series of proven rules for our everyday lives. Although they developed from my involvement in the financial world, they have proved to be a wonderful aid on the path to self-realization.

The law of yin and yang

Every exaggerated endeavor in one direction automatically brings with it an opposing effort. This is the eternal interplay of the life forces. When we become involved in it and make use of the knowledge about it, things will go well for us.

The law of personal responsibility

Instead of asking who can solve our problems for us, we should ask how we can obtain the knowledge and abilities to do this for ourselves.

The law of love

If we make the effort to act in a way that benefits all participants, open up to the guidance of God as well as we can, and dispense with the assertion of our will (but not the satisfaction of our needs), our lives will never be poor. We will always receive what we really need to live well.

The law of the power of self-knowledge

The fears, the greed, and the talents that we can perceive and love within ourselves—we can also perceive and love these in other people. Everything that we can perceive and love is our faithful friend and helper in mastering our problems in life. Whatever we don't want to recognize and love will always be in our way. And we can't run away from it because it is a part of us.

The law of unbiased knowledge

If we make the effort to thoroughly understand the world and ourselves in an unbiased manner, we will always have helpers who give us what we can't achieve for ourselves in this process. The knowledge gained in this manner will never leave us and makes it possible for us to progress more easily on our path, be successful, and give us other important assistance in our process of self-realization. If we look for a prefabricated system of understanding that we believe we can simply assume, we miss out on our own uniqueness and let our talents atrophy. Lasting success and happiness will not happen since these are dependent upon our striving for our own knowledge. Instead, we can use the knowledge of others as stimulation for our own growth.

The law of fair exchange

Nothing ever comes to us without a corresponding return service. This isn't bad since in this way we can participate in the treasures of the world and others participate in our unique abilities. Each becomes richer through a fair and conscious exchange! The only catch in this is that we must perceive and accept the return service. If we have fixed ideas about what we want, we won't be able to make the best of things and will carelessly throw away the riches that were almost in our hands. And then we will naturally remain poor and complain about the evil world that gives us nothing without a constant battle. How should it when we are usually reaching for something that is meant for someone else instead of accepting our own gifts? When we attempt to always get more than we give, we will receive much that we can't use because our attention is basically on the quantity and not the quality. We will often be presented with the bill for this abundant attention when we least expect it and don't want it. The universe doesn't let itself be deceived. It balances all the accounts equally in the end.

The law of the proper time

There is a proper time for everything that we do. The schedule lies within us. Only we can see and truly understand it. If we make the effort to use this plan and do everything at the right time for it, we will be successful. But we will miss out on the opportunity of the proper moment if we don't accept this law. We can try to feel what the universe wants us to do now and gather our experiences in small things so that we become secure enough for the big ones. We can recognize whether we are doing the right thing at the right time when we feel good while doing it, are successful, find unexpected support, and prove to have more talent than we ever believed we had. This is how it feels when we swim with the flow of life! Our work bears rich fruits almost without any effort. When we recuperate from it, we have a sense of well-being, are deeply relaxed, and experience new strength.

The law of anti-cyclic behavior

According to the above-mentioned law of yin and yang, every exaggeration results in a new, contrary movement. This means that the universe gathers all the forces and uses them to set a new cycle into motion at the end of a cycle. If we help in this process by concentrating our powers on the balance of the extremes, the universe will reward us more than enough for our services since we are promoting the flow of life with our efforts. If we understand this law, we understand meaning and holistic success from the cosmic standpoint. God only has the hands of human beings who want to work with Him in order to do His works on this earth. It's up to us to choose God and live in the light.

Chapter 8

SELF-FULFILLMENT— THE GUARANTEE OF A RICH LIFE

How can we be successful and happy at the same time? It's really quite simple...

Design Our Lives like a Work of Art

Every human being is unique. Each of us has different, wonderful talents, the development of which represents a blessing for us all. This also applies to you, as well as every other human being. No matter who we are, where we come from, what kind of education we have, how old we are, how we look – each of us have inherited the possibility of creating wonderful things that no one else can accomplish. We can design our lives like a work of art when we live what we are. When we allow ourselves this, we finally no longer have to hide behind a disguise. Much energy, that otherwise would have been bound up in our various masks with which we have pretended to ourselves and our fellow human beings that we are someone else, will become available to us. We can stop being the way we think other people would like us to be. If we stop doing it *now*, we can unpack the presents that have been slumbering unused and ignored within us for so long.

Each of us is wonderful and everyone needs our abilities!

Or does this just apply to some people but not to others? Are there exceptions to this? No! It really applies to each and every one of us.

Push the Stones of Normality from Your Heart

The stones of normality weighing on our heart are what block the path on the street to success and happiness through self-realization. Let's throw them off at last! We are the only ones who cling to them and stop them from falling off. How can we do this? Our heart, more precisely, our heart chakra*, is the source of your ability to love and therefore also your ability to accept yourself as you are. In the course of your life, many thought patterns hostile to love have been laid upon your heart center by your parents, teachers, relatives, friends, and other role models. The source of your love energy has been so dammed up that at some point after the one-thousandth "be like this and that!," "do this, don't do that!," "people aren't supposed to behave like that!," "be sensible and live like a normal person!," we no longer know or perhaps don't even want to know who we *really* are because of a fear of not being loved and accepted by others.

But this is no longer the situation! Now that we are adult, strong, and responsible, we can shelve this obstructing pattern and learn to live our wonderful uniqueness. The following exercises can help us achieve this goal:

Exercise I—Freeing Your Heart

Get comfortable and listen to your breathing until you are calm and relaxed. In front of your inner eye, imagine your heart. Ask to see all the energy patterns hostile to love and standing in the path of your self-fulfillment in the form of stones piled up on your heart. Look at the heap of rubble for a moment and be conscious that you will soon begin clearing them away. This can and will let your heart once again beat freely and radiate love within you and around you. Wait until you have the feeling that it's the right point in time. You will clearly recognize it because of the intense inner need to take action. Then ask God, or whatever you call the creative force, to help you in doing this important work. Now inhale and exhale deeply a few times. Perceive how large amounts of love energy are drawn into your body in the process and how good this feels. When

---

* There is a description of how the heart chakra functions in the Appendix 2.

you have the feeling that enough power has flowed into you, exhale strongly and clap your hands at the same time. Then vigorously rub your palms together, continuing until you feel a strong tingling or vibrating in them.

Now visualize a pillar of radiant light that leads from your heart to the source of all being, to God. Then place both of your hands the place where your heart beats. With your inner eyes, watch how a great amount of light and love flows from your hands to your heart. Feel the powerful vibrations and observe how stone after stone is flung off your heart, slowly at first and then with increasing speed, disappearing into the pillar of light. They will all unite with the source of creative power on a high subtle level and turn back into love. Once all the rocks have gone into the light, close the light pillar through the power of your thoughts. Let more energy flow from your hands into your heart chakra for a while longer in order to fill the empty places with the power of love. This is very important: Don't forget to do it! You need this to prevent new rocks from forming. When you are done, remove your hands. Take a few deep breaths and open your eyes.

Exercise II—Freeing Your Personality

The following exercise should always be done in connection with Exercise I. This deals with freeing the solar plexus chakra, the energy center that organizes the personality, feelings, and power ability. If this is strongly blocked because of a deep sense of powerlessness and its related fears, it isn't possible for us to be at peace within ourselves and follow our path in a self-assured and powerful way.

The course of the exercise corresponds with the last exercise, with the exception that you ask to see the various fear patterns as rocks on the solar plexus chakra with your inner eyes and visualize the pillar of light above your solar plexus instead of your heart. The hands should be placed on your solar plexus to let the energy flow to it.

Exercise III—Inner Guidance

Here is something to help you in difficult situations when others direct a great deal of energy toward you because they absolutely want you to get off your own path. In these situations, it may be difficult for you to really feel how and where to continue.

Stand up straight. Your legs should be a bit bent and the tips of the toes pointing inward. Now spread your arms widely, as if you wanted to give someone a welcoming hug, and inhale deeply. While exhaling, bring your arms together and then place one palm on your forehead and the other palm on your heart. Leave it there for a while and feel how the energy flows into you. Inhale once more and open your arms widely, then bring them back together. This time, place the other palm on the forehead and the heart. Repeat this process until you feel a sense of security and perception grow within you. After the exercise, don't give any more thought to your problem but occupy yourself with something that you enjoy. Sleep on it for a night and wait to see what new possibilities your dreams or life will show you.

In general, this method works very well within one to three days. If you feel very confused or think that it wasn't enough the first time, repeat the exercise daily, at best in the evening, until you are successful with it. When doing this, it's important that you don't want to assert your will with a specific path. Give the universe the opportunity to take care of you and thankfully use what it sends you. And be certain that it will *always* place something that is meaningful in the holistic sense in your hands. However, you must grab hold of it.

Used as directed, this last exercise is very effective in activating important areas of the forehead chakra and heart chakra. This helps prepare us for our adventures on the path of self-discovery.

There's a Lot to Discover—Look Forward to It!

Exercise IV—Discover Your Talents with the Help of Your Inner Child

When your heart is finally free enough to let the love flow within you and into your environment, you only need to put these new possibilities to use. Now it's a matter of finding out what kind of talents you actually have. At the next opportunity, take 30 minutes and start with a relaxation exercise that you enjoy. Then return to your childhood in your thoughts. As soon as you can perceive yourself as a small child, ask this little person, your inner child, what it would like to do with the possibilities that you have as an adult. What games would it like to play? In its opinion, how should your life be so that it can feel good and happy? Then listen to what it tells you and be open for its message. Once it has told you everything it has to say this time (there should be additional times so that you become increasingly more familiar with this aspect of your personality), ask it to give you a sign when you do or say something in your everyday life that blocks its development. For example, this can be an itching or a vision of a wastepaper basket, into which you should put this behavior that is inappropriate for you. Be creative and think of something that is fun for both of you. Or let your inner child suggest something beautiful. Promise it—and therefore yourself—that you will be attentive and listen. Ask it not to take offense if you don't immediately know what it wants.

In your everyday life, pay attention to these warning signals and particularly to the spontaneous feeling of curiosity and fascination. Whenever it is at all possible, follow these impulses. As messages from your inner child, they are certain to lead you to the best possibilities for realizing your talents. Simply play along with it. It is a great deal of fun to play with the possibilities of an adult in life. In any case, since I've starting doing this I feel better than ever before. I have yet to experience anyone who has suffered harm from this attitude. Moreover, it helps you to again gain access to the power of the child. You think children aren't as powerful as adults? Actually, they're much stronger! Try imitating all the movements that a three-year-old or four-year-old child makes while playing for an hour. If you can keep up for half an hour, you're in really great shape.

Imagine that you had the strength of a child for self-fulfillment. Wouldn't that be fantastic? Well, now you know how you can get it as an adult. Only today you have much more knowledge and experiences that help you apply this strength in a practical way. Every great artist, every significant researcher—simply anyone who creates beautiful and valuable things—has found and maintained this connection to his or her inner child in at least certain areas of life. The unrestrained strength for self-fulfillment flows to us from this source, astonishing the people who are not "initiated."

Money Is Love in Action

This phrase is said to come from Findhorn, a spiritual community in northern Scotland. The nature of money was already discussed in detail in Chapter 1. This section deals with learning and training the correct, healing use of money and then making it available to others. Money is a fantastic tool for loving self-realization. You can achieve this in the following way...

Exercise V—Rich Forever Through the Power of Love

Write the following sentences on an attractive piece of paper:

"I request to always have as much money as I need in order to be able to learn everything that is important for me right now. In turn, I will gladly make my unique contribution to the growth of all things and respectfully, thankfully, and lovingly accept other people's contributions. I ask the powers of light and love to help me in the fulfillment of my promise."

Now take a silver dollar and fold it into the page you have just written on. In conclusion, write "Money Is Love in Action!" on both sides and breath on it a few times in order to connect your energy to it, pack it into a little cloth bag, and wear it around your neck or put it under your pillow at night. This amulet will help you fulfill yourself lovingly in your work, bringing a blessing for all those who are involved. Honor it and thank it now and then for the wonderful experiences that you will have in the time that follows.

Your Personal Program for Success and Happiness Through Loving Self-Fulfillment

Exercise VI—Attuning to the Cosmic Order

In a quiet moment, take a piece of paper and a pen. Write as comprehensibly as possible about how you imagine your future. Paint it in the loveliest colors and include everything that you want to have. Let all the castles in the air of your deepest longings take form on the paper. When you are finished, take another look to be sure that really everything has been included. Then take a few old newspapers and make a small fire out of them in an appropriate place. Take the paper that you have written on into both hands, lift it up to the sky, then slowly and consciously speak the following words:

"I sacrifice today and forever these, my personal wishes for the future and trustingly open myself for all the good that God will give me in abundance at the right time in order to enrich and fulfill my life, and that of everyone involved, with meaning. I trust in the power of light and love and ask it to guide me."

Then place your wishes, with the paper upon which they are written, into the flames and receive the many blessings for which you have now opened yourself. You can always repeat this ritual whenever you have the feeling of having become stuck in some kind of idea and want to open yourself once again to a trusting cooperation with the creative force.

Expect nothing, be ready, and you will receive everything!

The exercises in this chapter are simple. But don't underestimate them! Because of their special form and a blessing from the powers of light and love, they will let intense healing energy flow to those who do them every time. In order for them to be effective, it's not important to believe in them. But stick to their order and do them consciously.

Before each ritual, become very clear about why you want to do it. Take your time in doing it and don't plunge into some type of hectic activities afterward. The more often you gather experiences with these exercises, the more you will be surprised and pleased at their effects. Of course, what you have been secretly wishing for is usually not what happens. But you will receive something instead that in retrospect will prove to be much more satisfying for you and everyone involved.

The last ritual in particular will give you the opportunity to realize everything within you in the best way possible, supported by the cosmic order. If you give God the opportunity to help you, He will always say "yes" and help you wherever you let Him.

Much of this chapter may seem quite exotic and improbable to you. Because of our upbringing, we have all been imprinted with the pattern that we have to assert ourselves against a hostile world. So we all more or less expect to have a life full of struggle and problems. Yet, what costs us so much strength and produces conflicts is just the resistance against the flow of the life energy. When we try to swim against this current, it takes a lot of strength and we don't get very far, despite all the efforts we make. And at some point, when we are exhausted, it manages to drag us along with it. But then we can no longer enjoy it because of our exhaustion, fear, and bitterness about our failure and the loneliness we have chosen through our actions. We overlook the opportunities that it constantly offers to us. We should remember this: The brakes of a car wear down through the process of braking! So let's take our foot off the brakes. We have a built-in chauffeur who knows exactly where to go without having to brake.

If we trustingly surrender ourselves to the guidance of the life flow and take advantage of the tailor-made opportunities that continually cross our path, things will go well for us. This is our personal success program. It is better than any human brain could consciously dream up since it fairly and lovingly takes all interests into consideration. There just isn't anything more perfect than the divine order. So why shouldn't we be motivated enough to use our opportunities?

Chapter 9

HEALING THE MATERIAL CONSCIOUSNESS

What is the Material Consciousness?

This is the area of our personality from which we deal with money, our occupation, work in general, our possessions, the resulting demands and problems, perspectives for happiness, and the small and great joys of the world, among other things. It is the anchor of our existence and responsible for shaping our everyday life. If there are numerous blocks in the material consciousness, we will have difficulty in finding fulfillment in our life. We will repeatedly overlook that God is in the entire Creation. We will also neglect to include the flow of cosmic life energy in our thoughts and actions in the material realm.

If we open up to the spirituality of the *entire* Creation, God will always give us His hand. If we take it, we will have a very beautiful and meaningful time here on earth. The more we separate the Creation into "good" and "evil," the more difficulty we have in being holistically successful. We need to learn to see the spiritual quality, the spark of light, in everything. We can use it by helping with our efforts to let it shine brightly. Then we will experience every day as a gift. With every dollar that we spend, we allow love, consciousness, and spiritual energy to be radiated into the world. Everything that we buy with our money will make it possible for us to experience the love of our fellow human beings and the presence of God.

Then we will use our possessions as a portion of the divine Creation, for which we are responsible, in a meaningful way. We will maintain this portion respectfully, and increase it with a good conscience and success. We do this because we have recognized that the Creator has given us an opportunity to learn, to achieve self-perception and knowledge of God, to treat the world in a loving and responsible way, and to fulfill our needs with what we have.

The hours that we spend working will no longer be a burden and a waste of time. Instead, we can use our occupation for self-realization and developing our talents. Others will participate in what we have worked on through the economic cycle. We will be proud of what we pass on since the work has been done as an expression of our wonderful uniqueness with love, consciousness, and respect for the Creation.

The previous chapters dealt extensively with these areas of life and our attitude toward them. In closing, here is a program that will help us approach the material world in an increasingly harmonious way.

Learning Steps for a Healing Approach to the Material World

Exercise 1: Meaningful and Satisfying Work

Every evening, take a few minutes to become aware of what you have created that day through your capacity for work. Close your eyes and first let all the images of disappointment and frustration appear that have collected during this day. Just look at them, but don't evaluate them. Allow them to come—and go. Finish this part of the exercise by saying out loud:

"I ask for the ability to shape or understand everything that has taken away the joy of working from myself, and all the others who are involved in my work, in such a way that it will make us feel good and fill our lives with joy and meaning. I ask for the strength to cast aside all work situations that I can't change in a positive manner. Instead, I want to receive those that are meaningful and create happiness. I want to learn to use them the right way."

Now take a few deep breaths, letting the tension and disappointment flow out of you with each exhalation. Visualize these disharmonious energies as a dark liquid. With each inhalation, take in joy and satisfaction in the form of crystal-clear, refreshing liquid until you feel balanced.

Now visualize how the products of your work go to other people and help them by enriching and supporting their lives. Each day, attempt to bring further meaningful aspects of your work into your consciousness. At the end of this part of the exercise, say out loud: "What I have done is good, and I thank God for the ability to be able to do it."

This little exercise almost works wonders when you do it on a regular basis. It trains your consciousness and helps you to assume responsibility for your working life. It will help you find joy and meaning in it.

Exercise 2: Working on Money with Light—Spiritual Environmental Protection

When you take cash, checks, money-transfer forms, or credit cards, anything that resembles money, into your hands in order to spend it or receive it as a return service, think of the three important words: love, respect, thankfulness. This may perhaps seem difficult, but try it out. This exercise will change your life. All the material things that come from you will be spiritually charged with these three energy qualities. Nothing will be able to block their effects. When they are used with consciousness and understanding, they summon the highest spiritual power, God.

Everything that you accept and give away will be harmonized as a result, no matter what kind of emanation it had before. So you can make your contribution to the healing of society, and help yourself and your fellow human beings, by bringing harmony into the world. This is spiritual environmental protection! Our era is sick because of a lack of meaning, because of the rejected, forgotten connection to the source of all being. If we consciously recreate this relationship and charge material things with the universal creative power, then the earthly world can be connected to the divine meaning of life once again. We could say that this is a contribution to letting the Age of Aquarius begin more quickly and with less difficulties.

Exercise 3: Consciousness of Wealth

Write down what you possess. Get yourself an attractive notebook or ring binder and list everything that belongs to you. Include things you have rented and which you have a right to use. Be very precise.

Write down as much as possible. Take an inventory of your material goods. The first time you do this, it may take a while to complete. But this is important consciousness training! If you don't know what you have, you can't formulate any practical thoughts about its meaningful use, responsibility, holistic wealth, and so forth. Then write down the material value in dollars behind each item. It isn't important to figure it out down to the last penny. However, the estimation should be very realistic. At the conclusion, add it all up. You will be surprised at how rich you are! Up to now, I have never known a person who could estimate the actual value of his or her possessions in this exercise.

Now read every point of the list loud and clear. When you are finished with all of it, say slowly and consciously: "I have received all of this through God's help and my accomplishments. It has been entrusted to me to fulfill my material needs, to recognize and develop my talents. This is how I can learn love, respect, and thankfulness and spread them throughout the world. I will do my best for all involved to meaningfully use and care for my possessions. When I no longer need something, I will exchange it for different goods that are important for me. Or I will give it to someone who can use it. Only when it truly no longer is useful will I throw it away, thank it for the service that it has given me, and ask that it once again become a useful part of the Creation. May God help me in fulfilling this resolution in my life!"

This exercise will probably be too extensive to complete in one attempt. You are so rich that your possessions can't even be recorded within a few hours. Don't worry about this. Make several attempts— but be sure to do it.

Later, work on healing your material consciousness about once a month. Add to the list anything that you have acquired in the meantime. This naturally means striking what you have exchanged, given away, or thrown out. When doing this, think of Exercise 2!

Exercise 4: The Spiritualization of Your Material Consciousness

This exercise concerns the moral evaluation of your material possessions. In concrete terms: There will be many material goods that you have learned to classify as beautiful, meaningful, proper, and good. And there will be others that you evaluate as ugly, absurd, false, and bad. As long as you think this way, you are not taking seriously your responsibility toward the Creation and aren't truly in the position of living love and spreading it to others. "Good" and "bad" is the work of human beings. What do you think of the following opinion?

No object in the world is bad except when people treat it as
something bad.

The human being decides whether he wants to use a hammer to attach a picture to the wall or smash in another person's skull. The human being can choose whether he uses a knife to commit murder or to clean and cut vegetables. But wait! In the last case, he ends the life of the bell pepper or tomato. Is this bad? If we assume that life never ends but just takes on another shape, the death of a being on one level of existence is the precondition for birth on another. Before we were conceived, we also had to die to the subtle world. There is no life without death, and no death without life.

This thought is conveyed in a song of the spiritual American Indian tradition:

"Hoof and horn, all that dies shall be reborn.
Corn and grain, all that's cut shall rise again!"

In these examples, it isn't all that hard to set the accustomed valuations into a different perspective. This is how we achieve a new, more holistic understanding of them. This process of examining our judgments is very important in order to dissolve obstructing thought patterns and make way for a loving, spiritual view of the world. Nothing is meaningless! However, it is an essential task for each of us to do what we can in order to discover the hidden meaning—the divine light in the ten-thousand things of the world, as the Chinese call the diversity of the Creation, and use it accordingly for the benefit of everyone involved.

Here is the actual exercise:

Get yourself a daily newspaper and select a larger or smaller number of words, according to whatever suits you, that you have learned to judge in a negative manner. In a few sentences, write down your negative valuation of them and give brief reasons for them. Now try to discover the hidden divine meaning in each of the words by examining the following points:

Is your opinion based on a

Generalization?

This means that you believe, for example, that all insurance agents are crooks who want to extract money from your wallet for superfluous things? Do you know "all insurance agents"? Be aware that your conclusions are based on limited experiences. Therefore, they probably don't correspond to reality.

Has your opinion been created through a

Distortion?

Do you possibly have a personal prejudice against insurances and their agents because you or people close to you have had bad experiences with them or have passed their opinion about them onto you? Perhaps you are also afraid of cases of loss, the future, and dealing with money at all and this has caused you to have a negative judgment. Examine whether

> *fears*
> *greed*
> *envy*

have caused you to form this opinion. Be honest!

Is your assessment caused by a

Deletion?

Have you disregarded certain information that could give you a different attitude because you didn't like the way it was conveyed. For example, did someone who you don't like or who you think is incompetent say it or was it written in a newspaper that you find to be "bad"?

Then look for a constructive meaning in every word that can give you an indication of the holistic, complete sense of this term. Don't stop until you get closer to this meaning. By the way, it can always be found since the world is a meaningful creation of God.

When we human beings recognize and understand the holy MEAN-ING in every thing, love, fulfillment, and wealth will be spread throughout the world. We have the freedom to deal with everything in our life in a meaningful or meaningless way.

Liberating Your Shadow Aspects

If you still haven't found a holistic attitude toward something, then use the

Devil's Advocate Principle

In anything that occurs to you, advocate exactly the opposite of your previous opinion. In this way, you can very quickly get to know the relativity of a value judgment. Make a game of letting the best possible argument occur to you for this purpose. You can also do this exercise with friends. It is quite fun to be completely different for once and experience people you know from an opposite perspective. Moreover, it makes you more tolerant, loving, and creative to occasionally slip into the role of a person with an opposing opinion. I also call this process liberating your shadow aspects: Whatever you most defend yourself against—and feel anger, fear, aversion, and repulsion toward—is also *always* connected with an unlived, unloved portion of your own personality. This may be a talent that appears bad to you because you haven't lovingly accepted it and haven't experienced its divine meaning, which *always* exists.

The more shadows you accept within yourself and in the outside world, the more loving and happy you will be. Consequently, there is increasingly less for you to be afraid of and against which you must fight, so it is worth taking this path. And if you think this is all far too much: If you just do one exercise, you have already opened your heart a little bit. Focus on your feelings after the exercise. You will clearly perceive how good you feel and that you have a little more unity and love within you.

However, even if you don't indulge in anything else, at least allow yourself to experience love. It isn't fattening, but it is very healthy!

Appendix 1

INSTRUCTIONS FOR THE PENDULUM TABLES

Basic Information on Using the Pendulum, Please Read Carefully Beforehand

The pendulum tables are meant to help you systematically tackle problems and find ideas for harmonizing your life in a simple and effective manner. Since it's impossible to include all the alternatives in the tables, I've added additional tables without any entries to the standard tables 1 to 11, which have proved to be effective in the practice for me. You can design these blank tables to suit your needs.

On all the tables, you will find a field for errors. This is very important. Your pendulum will swing to this field when there isn't an appropriate answer on the table or when you shouldn't expect any meaningful results from working with the pendulum at this time for other reasons. With Table 1, the "Error Correction Table," you can then more closely determine the error. If you want to work with the pendulum on a matter that is very important to you, then ask time and again whether the results are accurate. In case of doubt, ask someone else who works with the pendulum and isn't emotionally connected with the topic. Additional perception work with the I Ching, Tarot, or similar synchronistic oracles can also be recommended in order to further exclude errors and receive the broadest possible approach to the respective problem.

If you have never worked with the pendulum in a serious way or have very little experience with it, it is best to attend a good seminar on the topic and/or read more extensively about it.*

Also see my "Pendulum Healing Handbook", published by Lotus Light/Shangri-La in 1998.

Explanations on the Pendulum Tables

Pendulum Table 1 (Error Correction)

This table offers you the frequent causes for a wrong answer by the pendulum. The entries explain themselves for the most part, except for the alternative of "Not permitted to answer at this time." This statement means that an answer wouldn't be in the sense of the cosmic order right now. There are situations that we must go through with as much self-determination as possible, building only on our own ability to judge in order to learn personal responsibility and trust in the direct guidance of God. It is also possible that in the holistic sense this information could have harmful effects on those involved in the situation.

Pendulum Table 2 (Major Chakras)

You can use this table for a variety of purposes. For example, you can quickly and reliably determine which chakra is affected by a specific problem. Then you can consult a good chakra book (see Bibliography) and do the corresponding exercises to strengthen and harmonize these energy centers. If you would like to know from which chakra you (or someone else) mainly function at this time, the table is also very useful for this purpose. However, you shouldn't turn this approach into a hierarchy – "*He* is still living from the root chakra, but *I'm* already at the heart center." Each chakra is equally important in the process of self-development, and you can strengthen your heart chakra in a very practical way by giving up your prejudices and approaching your fellow human beings in a loving manner. Thinking in hierarchical structures (he/she is better/worse than me) kills love and makes it impossible for us to develop toward the light since *all* colors are represented equally in white light. If certain colors are emphasized, then the light is no longer white but colored.

In the case of conflicts, you can determine which chakras are harmonious in the relationship and which are imbalanced. If you have financial difficulties, you can use the pendulum to determine which chakra is blocked and promotes the problem. If you would like to do something in particular or if there is something you are afraid of doing, you can use the chakra table to find the energy center from which the motivation for the action originates. In this way, you can achieve clarity about your inner life and shape your way of living in a more conscious manner.

Pendulum Table 3 (Occupation)

The entries explain themselves for the most part. There is more detailed information on this topic in Chapter 4, "The Spiritual Meaning of an Occupation."

Pendulum Table 4 (Possessions)

The entries explain themselves for the most part. There is more detailed information on this topic in Chapter 5, "The Spiritual Meaning of Possessions."

Pendulum Table 5 (Money)

The entries explain themselves for the most part. There is more detailed information on this topic in Chapter 1, "The Spiritual Meaning of Money."

Pendulum Table 6 and 7 (Healing the Material Consciousness)

The entries explain themselves for the most part. There is more detailed information on this topic in Chapter 9, "Healing the Material Consciousness."

Pendulum Table 8 (Money Types)

This is a character-oriented typology. The entries and use of the tables is explained under "Money Types" in Appendix 2.

Pendulum Table 9 (Percent Values)

How to use this table is explained under "Money Types" in Appendix 2. You can also use this table to determine what portion of a certain chakra is involved in a specific problem or to what extent your subconscious mind accepts a certain solution to a problem (0% = anything else would be better: 100% = best possible idea). For example: You want to learn an occupation. Your choice is between a) systems programmer, b) pastry-cook, or c) mailman. You ask your pendulum to show you the "percent values" for every occupation to tell you how sensible the respective occupation would be when considering all the relevant circumstances (meaning from a holistic perspective) by using Pendulum Table 9. You receive 30% for a), 80% for b), and 10% for c). Now you know that a) and c) wouldn't be the right paths for you, but b) would be a good choice. If you want to find even better alternatives, test additional occupations with your pendulum.

Pendulum Table 10 (Yin/Yang Relationship)

With the help of this table, you can find out whether the energy qualities of an object to be examined, such as a chakra, tend more in the direction of yin or the direction of yang. "0" means a balanced relationship between yin and yang. "100" yin means pure yin energy. "100" yang means pure yang energy.

Pendulum Table 11 (Frequent Character Blocks)

The use of this table is explained at the end of Appendix 2.

Pendulum Tables

Error Correction
Pendulum Table 1

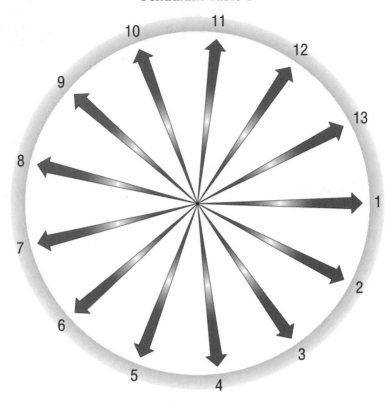

1 Outside disruptive influences	8 Not concentrated enough
2 Lack of trust	9 Too tired
3 Bias	10 Disruptive magical influences
4 Not seriously interested	11 Respect the privacy of others
5 Answer not on this table	12 Not permitted to answer at this
6 Vanity	time
7 Incompetence	13 Error

Major Chakras

Pendulum Table 2

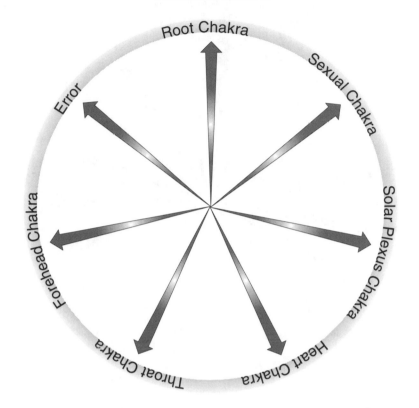

Error
1   Root Chakra
2   Sexual Chakra
3   Solar Plexus Chakra
4   Heart Chakra
5   Throat Chakra
6   Forehead Chakra

Occupation
Pendulum Table 3

1 Change occupation	13 Develop an emotional connec-
2 Change job	tion to your work
3 Change attitude toward work	14 Develop an emotional connec-
4 Do advanced training	tion to your colleagues
5 Accept the meaning of your	15 Develop an emotional connec-
work	tion to your business partners
6 Take a job on the side	16 Give up competitive way of
7 Advance your career	thinking
8 Give up your occupation	17 Develop loving ability to assert
9 Work more	yourself
10 Work less	18 Fulfill your individual task in
11 Learn a new occupation	the professional world
12 Develop more emotional	19 Error
distance to your work	

Possessions
Pendulum Table 4

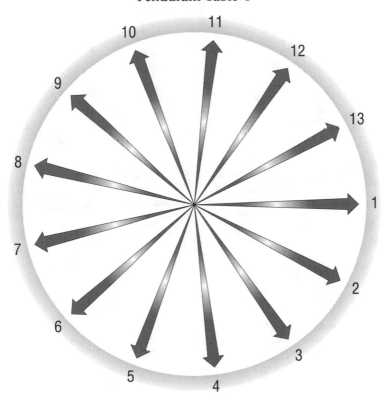

1 Understand holistic meaning of possessions
2 Accept possessions
3 Let go of possessions
4 Share possessions
5 Lovingly defend possessions
6 Take care of possessions
7 Use possessions
8 Develop emotional connection to your possessions
9 Develop more emotional distance to your possessions
10 Develop attitude of wealth
11 Develop gratitude for possessions
12 Increase your possessions
13 Error

Money
Pendulum Table 5

1	Understand holistic meaning of money	
2	Let money flow	
3	Make meaningful use of money	
4	Use money for yourself	
5	Give away money	
6	Learn to accept money	
7	Collect money	
8	Earn money	
9	Accept new possibilities of earning money	
10	Understand meaning of wealth	
11	Understand meaning of poverty	
12	Spend money with gusto	
13	Treat money in a loving way	
14	Learn to play with money	
15	Error	

Healing the Material Consciousness

A) Learning Steps
Pendulum Table 6

1 Learn to accept things	11 Understand your unique talents
2 Learn to give things away	and use them lovingly
3 Learn to engage in a fair	12 Learn to share responsibility
exchange	13 Learn humility
4 Resolve greed	14 Learn modesty
5 Resolve repulsion	15 Recognize and accept your own
6 Live personal responsibility	strength
7 Live life with gusto	16 Recognize and accept God's
8 Accept your personal power	help in your life
9 Accept differences	17 Error
10 Live creatively	

Healing the Material Consciousness

B) Recognizing and Resolving the Shadow
Pendulum Table 7

1 I'm not worth anything	14 Work must be strenuous
2 I'm incapable	15 Money is dirty
3 My life is meaningless	16 You're only worth something if
4 Other people define my life	you own something
5 I don't want to have power and	17 I don't know enough
exercise it	18 I'm stupid
6 I'm unimaginative	19 People are not receptive to what
7 I'm not strong enough	I have to give
8 I can't learn well	20 I'm too old or too young
9 There are good and bad people	21 No one helps me
10 Other people want to harm me	22 I'm untalented
11 I always receive too little	23 Karmic burdens block my life
12 I'm not lovable	24 I must help others
13 I can't permit myself any joys	25 Error
in life	

Money Types
Pendulum Table 8

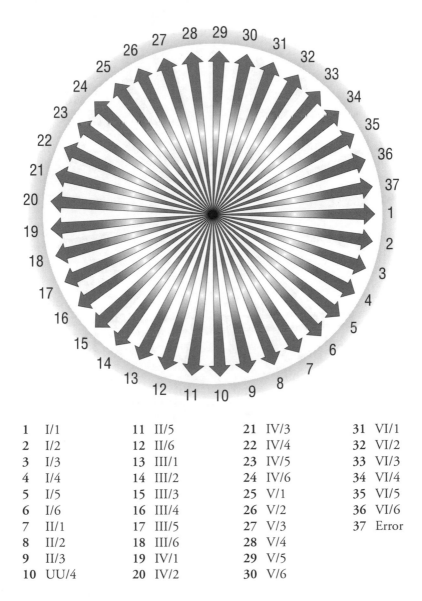

1	I/1	11	II/5	21	IV/3	31	VI/1
2	I/2	12	II/6	22	IV/4	32	VI/2
3	I/3	13	III/1	23	IV/5	33	VI/3
4	I/4	14	III/2	24	IV/6	34	VI/4
5	I/5	15	III/3	25	V/1	35	VI/5
6	I/6	16	III/4	26	V/2	36	VI/6
7	II/1	17	III/5	27	V/3	37	Error
8	II/2	18	III/6	28	V/4		
9	II/3	19	IV/1	29	V/5		
10	UU/4	20	IV/2	30	V/6		

Note: See "Money Types" on page 134 in Appendix 2 for explanation.

Percent Values
Pendulum Table 9

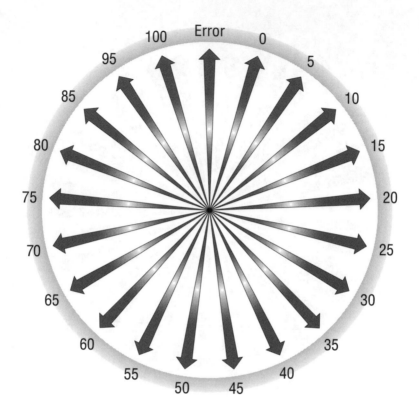

0   Minimum
100 Maximum

Supplementary Table B
(Yin/Yang Relationship)
Pendulum Table 10

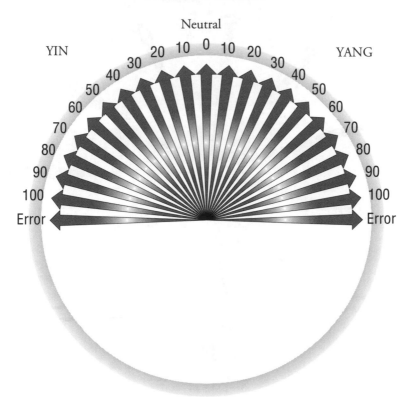

Frequent Character Blocks*

Pendulum Table 11

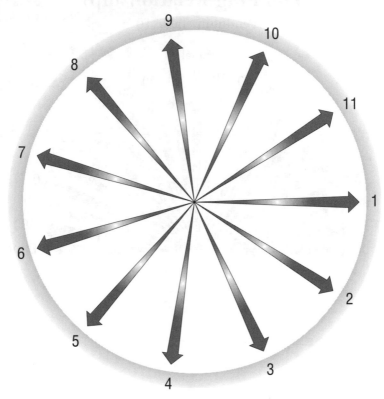

1	Harry (Harriet)Happy-Go-Lucky	6	Anita (Andy) Artist
2	Paula (Paul) Penny-Pincher	7	Nancy (Norman) Naive
3	Mark (Monica) Manager	8	Steve (Sonja) Specialist
4	Al (Alice) Atlas	9	Irene (Isaac) Idealist
5	Sammy (Sally) Survival	10	Sarah (Swen) Swindler
		11	Error

* Note: See Appendix 2, page 134ff., for explanations.

Your Own Pendulum Table

Topic ....

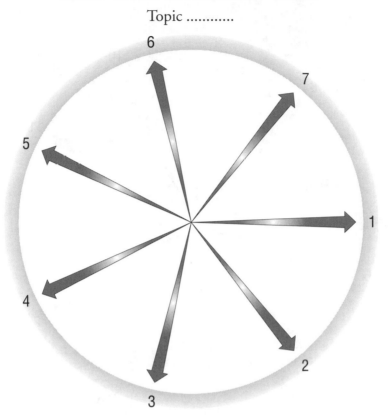

1 _____
2 _____
3 _____
4 _____
5 _____
6 _____
7 Error

Your Own Pendulum Table

Topic ....

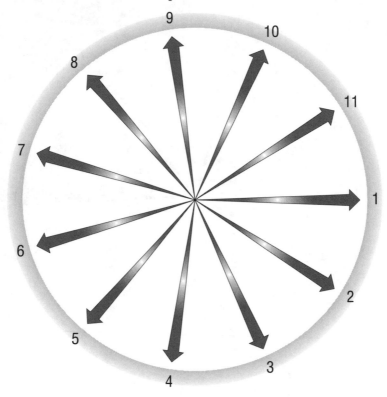

1	_____	7	_____
2	_____	8	_____
3	_____	9	_____
4	_____	10	_____
5	_____	11	Error
6	_____		

Your Own Pendulum Table

Topic ....

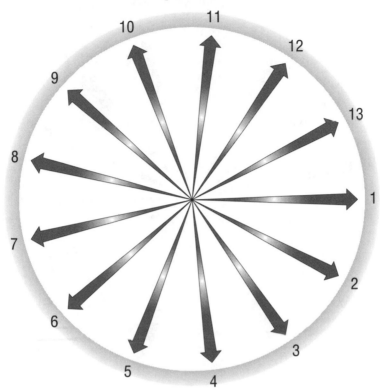

1	_____	8	_____
2	_____	9	_____
3	_____	10	_____
4	_____	11	_____
5	_____	12	_____
6	_____	13	Error
7	_____		

Your Own Pendulum Table

Topic ....

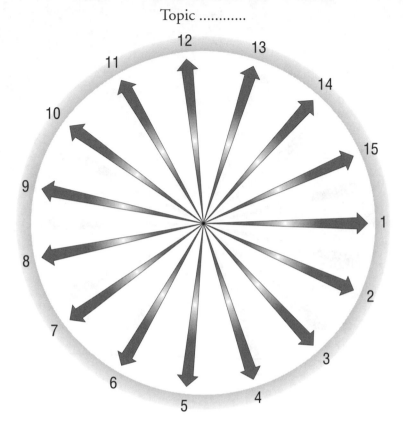

1	_____	9	_____
2	_____	10	_____
3	_____	11	_____
4	_____	12	_____
5	_____	13	_____
6	_____	14	_____
7	_____	15	Error
8	_____		

Your Own Pendulum Table

Topic ....

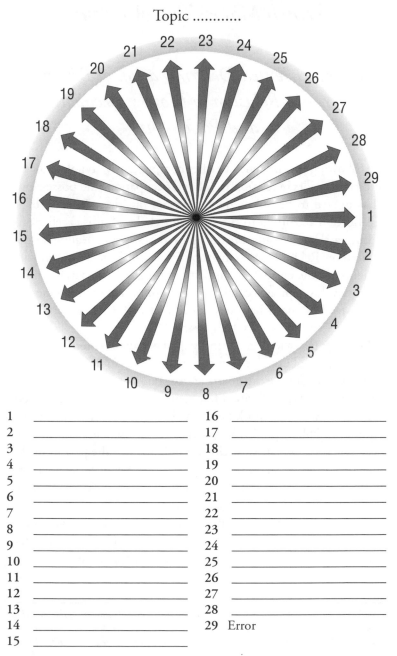

1	_____	16	_____
2	_____	17	_____
3	_____	18	_____
4	_____	19	_____
5	_____	20	_____
6	_____	21	_____
7	_____	22	_____
8	_____	23	_____
9	_____	24	_____
10	_____	25	_____
11	_____	26	_____
12	_____	27	_____
13	_____	28	_____
14	_____	29	Error
15	_____		

Which Money Type Are You?

Chakra-Oriented Determination of Behavior Patterns in Relation to Money, Occupation, and Possessions

The following text presents a rather comprehensive typology of the various behaviors in relation to money, occupation, and possessions. It has proved to be quite effective in my practice. Because of its classification according to the six major chakras*, it is excellent for creating a therapy using breathing exercises, yoga, healing stones, meditation, Reiki, or other methods that can have a harmonizing influence on the entire human being through these energy centers. Moreover, this approach can be directly connected with the method of aura-reading that I have developed and with chakra work based on the ancient Chinese I Ching oracle.**

Let's first take a look at the individual behavior patterns. You can do a little playful exercise to make them more comprehensible and lively for you. Simply categorize at least one person you know quite well with each type. Write a few sentences using concrete experiences to say why you think he or she is like this. Then consult the Pendulum Table 8 on "Money Types," and use the pendulum to check whether your subconscious mind also sees the person in this light. Try to understand deviating results as being supplementary. Find out in what situations which patterns tend to describe the behavior of such people in the right way. It is naturally rare to encounter someone in reality who embodies one of these money types in an unadulterated form. Most of us have portions of various characters within us that stand out or step back in certain situations.

---

* I don't use the seventh, the crown chakra, since its state is a type of summary of the conditions of the lower six major chakras.
** See "Aura Healing Handbook" by Walter Lübeck, Lotus Press/Shangri-La 2000

With Pendulum Table 9, "Percent Values," you can determine how the respective types dominate in a person under what kinds of circumstances. Please don't take the percent values as being too precise but interpret them as reference points. Remember that people emphasize various aspects of their character in different situations. Take into consideration that people can learn to change, expand, or limit their reaction patterns. A personality isn't a machine but constantly in a state of flux!

With Pendulum Table 10, "Yin/Yang Relationship," you can determine whether a chakra is charged with too much of the one quality or the other. Then look up this quality in the corresponding section of the chakra-oriented typology. With this knowledge, exercises can also be developed* in order to harmonize the yin/yang relationship within the corresponding energy system. After a cycle of exercises, you can determine the achieved success with the pendulum and Pendulum Table 10.

The Money Types and the Chakra-Oriented Oracle

The money typology can also be used like a chakra-oriented oracle system. For this purpose, get two different-colored dice. Designate one of these for determining the learning-topic chakra (see below for explanation) and the other for the area-of-experience chakra. Then write down a question that briefly and precisely outlines your problem. Also write down the date and your first and last name with it. It shouldn't be a "yes/no" question. Don't ask about more than one alternative at the same time like "what should I expect from my vacation in Spain, Italy, or South America?"

Here's an example of how to meaningfully ask a question: What situation should I expect in the first month at my new job?—How can my relationship with my partner be described?—How does my companion in life feel about me? What should be the energetic orientation of the appropriate occupation for me?—What situation

---

* For example, from Yoga, Polarity, Qi Gong, or Reiki.

should I expect if I get involved in a certain business deal?—What can I do to further develop myself?—What is the cause of my problem (give precise definition of problem)?

Now take both dice, think of your question, and shake them between your hands as in a game of dice until you have the feeling that it's enough. Throw them onto a smooth surface and then write down the number on top of each dice. Each of these will indicate one of the six major chakras. Now you only need to look for the two chakras (learning theme and area-of-experience chakra) in the typology (see pg. 139ff.). Read about it and come up with your own thoughts on the topic. If you use the pendulum to find the yin/yang energy value of the chakras, this will give you further indications of possible blocks.

Please don't abuse this system for power games with others or to put them down. Think how you would feel if an acquaintance applied his or her knowledge so unfairly against you. Instead, use it to understand yourself and others better so that you can participate in your own healing and their healing with total love and respect. Each of these chakra patterns describes a great talent that is worth developing because it is enriching for everyone involved when used in a harmonious and holistic manner. Always attempt to become aware of this ability and its great value, and then develop it.

Healing Blocks

The basic approach to healing blocked energies in the chakras consists of finding out which of the two energy centers involved (Pendulum Table 2) is disturbed and to what percent (Pendulum Table 9). Then work on harmonizing the one that is most disrupted with consciousness-expansion and energy exercises. A cause of disturbances that can frequently be found in the practice is an exaggeration of the yang or yin aspect of one or both chakras. In the case of yang, the following could also be used as a description: active, positive, masculine, productive, hard, hot, and dry. These terms could be used to describe yin: passive, negative, feminine, receptive, soft, cool, and moist. A brief description of the practical effects of a yang or yin energy that is too strong in each of the six main energy centers should help you recognize and work on these blocks.

This money typology is oriented upon the following pattern, which can be observed time and again: A person is occupied, mostly unconsciously, with learning the theme of the 2nd energy center, for example. We can call this theme the "learning theme." We can call the energy center that describes the qualities of this learning theme the "learning-theme chakra." In this case, it means that someone would like to have experiences in the area of joy in life and relationships in the broadest sense.

However, he may frequently select a completely different area in life in which to work on this theme. We can call this realm the "area-of-experience" chakra. For example, he can select the experiential realm of the 5th chakra, which organizes self-expression, creativity, and the artistic aspects of a human being, in order to learn about the theme of joy in life and relationships. Perhaps he plays a musical instrument (self-expression) together with others (relationship) in an orchestra as a hobby and enjoys expressing their moods by playing music (joy of life in self-expression).

In the reverse case, when someone has the 5th energy center as the learning-theme chakra and the 2nd as the area-of-experience chakra, she would like to learn self-expression in the area of joy in life and relationships. This constellation can be translated into action by the respective person learning to express herself in her typical manner (self-expression) as the clown (joy in life) in an amateur drama group or as a professional.

Play with this system a bit and attempt to find your own examples of the individual constellations of the chakras. When you use your ideas on this in practice, you can quickly find out whether they were correct or not. Many life situations basically offer opportunities for living out a number of combinations. It usually depends on whether the respective person becomes aware of what energies are suitable for him, as well as what opportunities for their realization are offered in their current life circumstances. This is preferable to giving up because it presumably isn't possible to use the existing area more appropriately. However, a more or less radical change in life's circumstances is sometimes also the better remedy. In any case, extensively examine all the alternatives before you burn any bridges that may still be of good service to you.

The following rules for interpreting certain chakra combinations have been confirmed time and again in my practice. I would like to give them to you to make your work easier:

People who have two of the same numbers in the chakra combination, such as I/1 or II/2, in relation to a question will appear quite prepossessed and biased to you in this respect. If you are advising them, you must adapt yourself very much to their way of thinking, feeling, and acting because they can't quite open up to approaches that are genuinely new. Through the combination of the same energies, they don't have a very broad range of choices available in mastering their learning experiences. This can be a true challenge for an advisor. Yet, you can learn to put your own will in its place and develop harmonious solutions in a creative manner from whatever exists.

The further the two chakras are apart, such as VI/1, the more open-minded and creative such people will generally be in approaching paths that are truly new for him or her.

If the information is related to the lower chakras, 1 to 3, this will always be a situation that urgently needs to be clarified in a constructive manner, even if the affected person sees this differently at that moment. These energy centers form the roots of human existence. If they are severely damaged, there are serious problems. So be particularly careful and attentive here.

Note: Roman numerals and Arabic numbers are used in the following descriptions of the various combinations of learning-theme and area-of-experience chakras. For example, I/2 describes the constellation with the 1st energy center (1) as the learning theme and the 2nd energy center (2) as the area of experience.

A Description of the Six Major Chakras in Relation to the Money Typology

1st Learning Theme or Area of Experience: 1st Chakra
(Base of the Spine Center)
— Structure and Survival —

Survival in the broadest sense; fleeing and fighting; preservation of the species through reproduction (need for an heir); preservation of the nation, the family to which a person feels he or she belongs; the elemental force of life (kundalini energy); the anchor of the human being in the material world; the inner structure; the form.

In the mental realm: fixed principles according to which a person lives; morals, ethics, and obeying laws in the most worldly form; orientation toward social norms and values ("people don't do that, everyone should do this") or what we consider them to be.

In the emotional realm: fixed ritual ways of behaving in which the feelings are expressed (wearing black to signify mourning, flowers on the wedding day, gifts for the birthday, etc.); the survival instinct in all its varieties.

In the physical realm: the skeleton as the structure-giving part of the body and blood as the bringer and storage means for a person's vital power.

Examples of structure-oriented and survival-oriented occupations: craftsman, behavioral therapist, minister, administrator and public official in the broadest sense, soldier, martial-arts teacher.

If the chakra is too *yang oriented*, such people will tend to try building and maintaining structures, no matter whether they are meaningful or not. Without structures of any type, they are afraid of losing stability. A lack of structure, disorder, and a desire to not fight appear false and antagonistic to them. Consequently, they will attempt to fight against them to assert order and a readiness for action. They think that anarchism is the greatest evil and are afraid of it. On the other hand, they feel secure and in good hands within a hierarchy.

If the chakra is too *yin oriented*, such people will tend to find it better to live in chaos, in a lack of structure. Fighting will appear to be rather meaningless to them, and they will attempt to avoid confrontations or will react hysterically in conflicts since they are lacking inner support. This solid structure is required for them to assert, defend, or calmly negotiate their standpoint in a secure and self-confident manner. The more impressively they experience another person's structure, the more they will become afraid of it. They will complain about "the state" or "the society" and feel secure and free in anarchy.

I/1 Chakra The theme of structure and survival is worked on in the area of experience related to structure and survival.

I/2 Chakra The theme of structure and survival is worked on in the area of experience related to relationships and the love of life.

I/3 Chakra The theme of structure and survival is worked on in the area of experience related to analysis, power, and digestion.

I/4 Chakra The theme of structure and survival is worked on in the area of experience related to unity and love.

I/5 Chakra The theme of structure and survival is worked on in the area of experience related to self-expression.

I/6 Chakra The theme of structure and survival is worked on in the area of experience related to perception.

IInd Learning Theme or Area of Experience: 2nd Chakra
(Lower Abdomen Center)
— Relationships and Love of Life —

Love of life and relationships in the broadest sense; sensual experiencing through touch; the joy of being alive; tenderness and sensitivity; games and fun; laughing and celebrating; erotic sexuality; singing and dancing; living with a community in the broadest sense; feeling and feelings; youthfulness.

In the mental realm: flexibility, tolerance, an ability to learn by being able to get involved, and a playful approach to the learning theme.

In the emotional realm: the complete range of feelings*, which are physically expressed and perceived spontaneously, naturally, and with much dynamism, but without overreacting; the perception of feelings in others and the reaction to them.

In the physical realm: everything liquid, soft, and flexible; particularly the urogenital system and the lower abdomen.

Examples of occupations that are oriented toward relationships and joy in life: introduction-agency work, entertainer, dance teacher, hotelier, social worker, clown, marriage therapist and sex therapist, Tantra teacher.

If the chakra is too *yang oriented*, such people will seek relationships and joy of life, seeing the meaning of life solely in them. They will avoid everything that they don't immediately think is fun or relationships that require work. They will tend to behave according to the motto: "The important thing is that I feel good!" He can't bear times without relationships and fun, and is very afraid of being alone and bored. As a result, he may frequently have several partners or quickly change companions when the relationship shifts from falling in love to the everyday phase with its strains. He attempts to experience the theme of this chakra by directing other people's attention to himself so that their life is fun. Eroticism, esthetics, pleasures of all types and keeping company with friends are essential for him.

If the chakra is too *yin oriented*, such people will tend to feel more secure without relationships and joy in life. Their fears make them lonely. As a result, they sometimes feel how they suffer and desire joy in their life. This perception frightens them and drives them to self-destructive actions, based on the desire to forget the inner pain through outer pain. They could be described as ascetics. However, we should differentiate between these people, who are ascetics because of fear and the ascetics who have the free choice of

---

* *Feelings make us capable of having relationships.*

living however they want but currently practice abstinence for significant reasons. The overly intensive yin orientation of the 2nd chakra can also be seen in a tendency to denounce pleasure, beautiful things, joy, and sensuality.

II/1 Chakra The theme of relationships and love of life is worked on in the area of experience related to structure and survival.

II/2 Chakra The theme of relationships and love of life is worked on in the area of experience related to relationships and love of life.

II/3 Chakra The theme of relationships and love of life is worked on in the area of experience related to analysis, power, and digestion.

II/4 Chakra The theme of relationships and love of life is worked on in the area of experience related to unity and love.

II/5 Chakra The theme of relationships and love of life is worked on in the area of experience related to self-expression.

II/6 Chakra The theme of relationships and love of life is worked on in the area of experience related to perception.

IIIrd Learning Theme or Area of Experience: 3rd Chakra
(Solar Plexus Center)
— Analysis, Power, and Digestion —

Analysis, power, and digestion in the broadest sense: sense of the self and feeling of personal responsibility; the ability to deal with stress; manipulation, contemplation, and being able to draw conclusions.

In the mental realm: logical thinking, the ability to process the sensory impressions.

In the emotional realm: being able to "digest" one's own and other people's emotional reactions, the ability to set limits, the assumption of responsibility, and trust.

In the physical realm: the digestion of food, the eyes as perceptive organs, and portions of the immune system.

Examples of occupations oriented toward analysis, power, and digestion: statistician, politician, nutritionist, manager, market researcher, cook, police officer, hypnotist.

If the chakra is too *yang oriented*, such people will tend to strive to amass power, manipulate others, and tend to be mentally oriented in their behavior. They very much enjoy analyzing and criticizing situations. They become fearful when they are powerless or helpless. To trustingly let go is a horror for them. This problem possibly expresses itself through sleep disorders and a lack of ability to fully surrender in the realm of sexuality. They don't like depending on others and attempt to always manipulate and keep other people under control according to their own wishes. They lovs technical things, they are so easy to assess. They don't like people who express their feelings; they show them aspects of their personality that they can't control. They feel secure when they are in the stronger position. They attempt to avoid situations in life where they can't be in control.

If the chakra is too *yin oriented*, such people will tend to be afraid of power, analysis, and digestion. It will be uncomfortable for them to influence others or perceive that they are being manipulated. They don't like to think about their experiences and tend to orient themselves more toward the idea of their feelings being the most important factor. They mistrust the rational mind and logic, as well as technology in all its forms since they feel that it limits their freedom. They like to be involved with individuals who engage them emotionally, even if these people take advantage of them afterward. When they learn, they retain and repeat the superficial knowledge when requested. Since they don't like to digest what they learn, the creative application of knowledge is usually closed off to them. In our current age, it's difficult for them to pursue their penchant for nature, animals, and clear circumstances in life with much freedom and harmony, and this can put them in a depressed mood.

III/1 Chakra The theme of analysis, power, and digestion is worked on in the area of experience related to structure and survival.

III/2 Chakra The theme of analysis, power, and digestion is worked on in the area of experience related to relationships and love of life.

III/3 Chakra The theme of analysis, power, and digestion is worked on in the area of experience related to analysis, power, and digestion.

III/4 Chakra The theme of analysis, power, and digestion is worked on in the area of experience related to unity and love.

III/5 Chakra The theme of analysis, power, and digestion is worked on in the area of experience related to self-expression.

III/6 Chakra The theme of analysis, power, and digestion is worked on in the area of experience related to perception.

IVth Learning Theme or Area of Experience:
4th Chakra (Heart Center)
— Unity and Love —

Unity and love in the broadest sense; harmony and synthesis; group feeling and group responsibility.

In the emotional realm: the feeling of inner connection with all manifestations of the Creation; compassion that doesn't mean suffering along with others but having sympathy for them; an ability to be responsible for other people, for groups, and for the environment.

In the mental realm: solving problems while fairly considering the interests of all involved; openness for the ideas of others based on the understanding that each of us only knows one part of the truth.

In the physical realm: the receptivity for nutrients, water, and environmental impressions of all types, as well as the ability to accordingly synthesize these with one's own needs.

Examples of occupations oriented toward unity and love: members of mediation commissions, politicians who strive for social unity and international understanding, all types of therapists, religious leaders who are more concerned with the well-being of people than the well-being of the church, and shamans as mediators of the unity between God and human beings.

If the chakra is too *yang oriented*, there will be a strong desire for unity, being accepted, and symbiosis. In extreme cases, such people will identify so much with some areas of their surrounding world that they no longer perceive their own individuality. This leads to an inundation with all types of stimuli, which are internalized without limitations. In turn, this overburdens the ability to analyze and synthesize and can lead to digestive disorders of a physical or energetic kind. The results are metabolic problems that develop in these areas. In the mental regard, various forms of psychoses can be created. Separation situations will stress such people, but everything that unites with them in some way gives them a sense of security and well-being. The excessive yang charging of this energy center is often the result of a separation situation that has been experienced in an extremely painful manner.

If the chakra is too *yin oriented*, situations in which unity is felt will be experienced as triggering fear. Such people will feel good when they can live in a very individualistic and separate manner. They detest a feeling of community or groups to which they should adapt themselves. The tendency toward separation can also be observed within them. They attempt to suppress all aspects of their personality that could produce feelings of unity. This is why they have little access to their emotional life and physical nature. If there has long been an overcharging of the yin quality of this energy center, schizoid ways of behaving will occur in a great variety of forms. A yin orientation that is too intense will often result from a long-lasting symbiotic relationship experienced in an extremely oppressive manner.

IV/1 Chakra The theme of unity and love is worked on in the area of experience related to structure and survival.

IV/2 Chakra The theme of unity and love is worked on in the area of experience related to relationships and love of life.

IV/3 Chakra The theme of unity and love is worked on in the area of experience related to analysis, power, and digestion.

IV/4 Chakra The theme of unity and love is worked on in the area of experience related to unity and love.

IV/5 Chakra The theme of unity and love is worked on in the area of experience related to self-expression.

IV/6 Chakra The theme of unity and love is worked on in the area of experience related to perception.

Vth Learning Theme or Area of Experience:
5th Chakra (Throat Center)
— Self-Expression —

Self-expression, facial expressions, and gestures; modulation and power of the voice; all types of preferences and dislikes; the personal manner of becoming ill; posture; artistic expression in all areas.

In the mental realm: the originality of deliberation and problem solving; the joy of thinking in an individual manner; esthetics in thought constructions and approaches to solutions.

In the emotional realm: the individual way of expressing feelings and esthetics in dealing with feelings.

In the physical realm: posture, facial expressions, and gestures; sound and volume of voice; physical form and build; being overweight, being underweight, or having normal weight; the personal way of becoming ill; addictions; esthetics in the approach to the body and physical being.

Examples of occupations oriented toward self-expression: artists of every creed and kind, all types of creative professions.

If the chakra is too *yang oriented*, there will be a strong tendency toward presenting oneself and one's uniqueness at all times and in all places. Self-expression becomes an end in itself. Everything must fit in with one's own opinions. Otherwise, it's wrong, ugly, and unfashionable. One's own opinions are naturally always right, beautiful, and appropriate. Self-realization is very important for these types of people. Even if others suffer as a result, they will try to drive them on. This type of block often results in inner loneliness, intolerance, and much conflict since their fellow human beings are limited in their own opportunities for self-portrayal and self-fulfillment through the this kind of person's excessive need for self-expression. People with excessive self-expression are well-suited for show business since they can finally really perform here. When they can sparkle and shine in their own way, they will be happy. They become fearful when their possibilities for expression are cut off or there is no audience for their performance. Their overly abundant energy needs a place where it can flow.

If the chakra is too *yin oriented*, such people will behave like the proverbial mouse. Sparing in facial expressions, gestures, and inflexible in terms of physical expression, they will have a quiet and monotonous voice, be dressed in an unimaginative manner, be unable to express what goes on inside of them, and display little creativity in what they do and think, and perhaps occasionally become conspicuous for this very reason. In the extreme case, this imbalance leads to a lack of relationships since relationships are largely based on self-expression. It also leads to a deep and painful feeling of futility in life*, despair, and a lack of vitality. Only through the process of expression and the reaction of the surrounding world do such people experience themselves and put themselves into perspective in relation to the rest of the world. Situations in which such people feel compelled to letting others participate in their inner life and individuality frighten them. They feel good when they don't have to present themselves or be conspicuous. This is embarrassing for them since they are deeply convinced of somehow being wrong or ugly.

V/1 Chakra The theme of self-expression is worked on in the area of experience related to structure and survival.

V/2 Chakra The theme of self-expression is worked on in the area of experience related to relationships and love of life.

V/3 Chakra The theme of self-expression is worked on in the area of experience related to analysis, power, and digestion.

V/4 Chakra The theme of self-expression is worked on in the area of experience related to unity and love.

V/5 Chakra The theme of self-expression is worked on in the area of experience related to self-expression.

---

* *This is also true since an essential meaning of our earthly existence is the enrichment of the world and our own being through creative and individual participation in the universal process of creation.*

VI6 Chakra   The theme of self-expression is worked on in the area of experience related to perception.

VIth Learning Theme or Area of Experience: 6th Chakra
(Forehead Center)
— Perception —

Perception, finding the way, and exploration (in terms of discovering correlations) in the broadest sense.

In the emotional realm: the correlation of recognizing and expressing feelings within the respective situation and through the individuality of the respective person; the broad spectrum of feelings that are perceived and experienced without limitations and previous reflection in accordance with the momentary situation.

In the mental realm: the orientation of thought toward comprehending the larger correlations and taking them into consideration when working out solutions to problems; the intuition as a higher level of processing information, without needing to analyze and synthesize.

In the physical realm: the unifying power that lets all the components of the organism meaningfully work together.*

Examples of perception-oriented occupations: philosopher and researcher; anyone whose task it is to understand correlations, solve problems through research, and help others on their path in life, etc.

If the chakra is too *yang oriented*, such people will attempt to explore everything that they get their hands on. In a virtually artistic manner, they will juggle with philosophical and esoteric theoretical models and become all wrapped up in further perfecting them. They are happy when they can research and perceive. They become frightened when practical matters are involved. They would rather study the Cabala for 10 hours than repair something on the car for

---

* *An intense block in this chakra can, for example, be expressed through cancer, meaning the independent proliferation of cells in the body that is not oriented toward the well-being of the entire body.*

10 minutes. They can theoretically do everything, but the practice is a horror to them. Being involved with reality is so uninteresting and meaningless. It is much more wonderful to reflect and understand the "Zen path of dishwashing" than to actually practice it.

If the chakra is too *yin oriented*, such people find it absolutely bothersome and superfluous to think about their place in the world. The actual practice is what counts and they feel at home there. Everything that they touch appears real to them and gives them a sense of security. Why should they torment themselves with theories and developing an understanding of the world when this doesn't bring any tangible benefits? They judge what is meaningful according to the practically applicable results. They are quite skeptical about activities that don't appear to have any direct relationship to reality. Why should they meditate when they could repair the leaky faucet during this time?

VII/1 Chakra The theme of perception is worked on in the area of experience related to structure and survival.

VII/2 Chakra The theme of perception is worked on in the area of experience related to relationships and love of life.

VII/3 Chakra The theme of perception is worked on in the area of experience related to analysis, power, and digestion.

VII/4 Chakra The theme of perception is worked on in the area of experience related to unity and love.

VII/5 Chakra The theme of perception is worked on in the area of experience related to self-expression.

VII/6 Chakra The theme of perception is worked on in the area of experience related to perception.

Frequent Chakra Blocks

In order to complete this system, I would now like to discuss some of the frequently occurring forms of blocked chakra patterns. There are naturally a great many more. You can learn much about yourself and others if you simply add further character types of your own and attempt to find out about the deeper cause of these imbalanced patterns. Once you have truly found the root of the problem, it will be easier to develop a healing approach (see below) to it. You can even make a game of this and play it with a few good friends. You will be surprised how many wonderful and creative solutions occur to the participants for the various character blocks. At the same time, you can also easily learn how to deal with your own character blocks.

One possibility for such a game is, for example, that one of the participants presents a character type with an appropriate name and story describing how he or she behaves. Then the next person uses an interesting incident to explain how this behavior has developed and which unsatisfied needs are probably at the root of the block. The next person then attempts to find an appropriate healing sentence.

The patterns can also be determined with the help of the Pendulum Table 11, "Frequent Character Blocks." You can develop approaches to releasing the congested energies by using the pendulum to determine which chakra is most intensely blocked. Then use the appropriate exercises from physical therapy and chakra-oriented energy work. A further possibility for harmonizing imbalances is working with the healing sentence included with each character type. You can use it in the following manner:

Say it loud and clear nine times before you go to sleep and listen within yourself for a moment after each repetition; or you can write it on a little note that you place somewhere in your home so that your eyes frequently fall on it; or say the sentence loudly and consciously and then immediately write a little story about it. Repeat this exercise every seven days and observe how your story changes with time.

By the way—the names you use should in no case describe the character qualities of real people you know.

1) Harry (Harriet) Happy-Go-Lucky

When he has money, he lavishly throws it around. If his wallet is empty, that's all right, there are always friends and relatives. Work? Now and then he does work a bit. But this tends to be participated in less instead of more. It ruins his enjoyment of life. It's much nicer to invite a few friends over for a party, go out and have fun, or drink a beer at his favorite bar. Is Harry unlikable? Actually, only when he is stubbornly hitting you up for money. Or when you try to analyze him or confront him with the more serious issues of life. Otherwise, he's a good host, drinking companion, party animal, charmer, and playmate.

Healing affirmation: I understand the deeper meaning of my life and fulfill it in order to enrich the world and myself.

2) Paula (Paul) Penny-Pincher

Her thoughts are mainly focused on how she can get something as cheaply as possible. Above all, she knows the price of everything and the value of nothing. When she can "damage" others by filling her plate to overflowing with the most expensive delicacies at the party buffet and stuffing everything into her mouth until she feels sick, she is still enormously pleased despite the stomachache. If she is offered something to drink, she only takes the best—and fills it up to the very top! As a host, she will hide the splendid wine (probably a birthday present since she would never buy it herself) in the cellar and instead buys discount beer to serve her guests. If she wants to attend a self-experience seminar, she will automatically look for the bottom price. Unless, of course, the speaker promises her a method of getting rich quick or safely hiding her money from the IRS, the "evil left", inflation, or similar catastrophes, in tax-exempt foreign countries. Then she's willing to pay something for the information, but still gnashes her teeth at the thought of the price. If she sells something, she will use all the tricks in the book to get as much money as possible for it—and still complain afterward that it was much too little.

Healing affirmation: The world takes care of me and I take care of the world.

3) Mark (Monica) Manager

"I don't have any problems, I solve them!" could be his motto. Money, possessions, and knowledge only mean something to him if he can use them to gain power. He doesn't cling to money but spends it when it helps him expand and solidify his realm of influence, both the private and the professional. He earns money so that he has it available for this purpose. No matter where he is, he succeeds in quickly and smoothly becoming the center of attention by capturing the attention of those who can be influenced until he has them adoringly at his feet. He makes recalcitrant individuals seem ridiculous, blackmailing them, or throwing them out in some other way. He's good at dealing with people since he knows what buttons to push so that they do what they should, or keep quiet out of fear. This is why he is also very interested in rhetoric, NLP, hypnosis, magic, positive thinking, and other strategies for success.*

Healing affirmation: My abilities have been given to me so that I can bring love into the world.

4) Al (Alice) Atlas

His joylessly pursed mouth occasionally allows a groan to escape. It's loud enough for the other people in his environment to notice it, but quiet enough so that no one can say he wanted to direct attention to himself with it. If he gives you something, the sound of his voice and his facial expression will let you know how much he had to work for it in order to give it to you. He feels that he accomplishes so much, endures mountains of responsibility without a complaint, hangs on when others would have long given up, a real man. Day in, day out he slaves away and toils for others (no, no, never for himself!). Although he never has asked "the others" whether they want him to sacrifice himself for them—and it's better that he doesn't since the response could possibly make him bitter—he knows very well that they would all starve, go broke, land in the gutter, or despair at the incomplete work if he didn't do it. A word of recognition now and then from his loved ones would be reward enough, but they don't even properly value his selfless drudgery. Well, maybe someone will at least build a monument to him after his death. If his fellow human beings avoid him at some point because they can no longer tolerate his sacrificial attitude or have taken advantage of him and then turned their backs on him, he will probably sigh: "Never

---

* I don't mean to devalue or judge the above methods. A tool is always just as good or bad as the person who uses it.

expect gratitude once you've served your purpose" or something else to that effect. It's probably difficult for him to believe that God and people can love someone who doesn't always have to work for it. And it's even more difficult for him to enjoy the love of the universe when he's working like a madman—he is usually in a terrible mood because of his exhaustion.

Healing affirmation: I am loved without having to work at it.

5) Sammy (Sally) Survival

Whether at work or in his private life, he is ready to take any risk. He finds security uninteresting, even the certain profit. It has to be Solomon's treasures that he finds after conquering the evil competitors, bloodthirsty beasts, and the dragons in front of the treasure cave. In the process, he will naturally also save a few kidnapped princesses and protect some poor orphans. He also likes to take risks in speculating on various markets that are as far away as possible. He bets on horses and greyhounds, parachutes, or does motocross. The main thing is that it's risky and he can prove what a great guy he is. Being friends with him can be fun. However, you probably won't remain one of his close companions for long if you don't drive used cars through the desert to the Congo, go on an expedition into the inner Amazon region to save the natives from civilization, or sail across the Atlantic in a collapsible canoe to prove that the Greeks actually discovered America. It's not that he would take it badly if you stayed at home. There aren't many fellows like him, but he just doesn't feel like going to the movies with you or doing a 9-to-5 job. Adventure calls and he's already running after it before the sound has a chance to fade away!

Healing affirmation: My strengths and my weaknesses are equally valuable and lovable.

6) Anita (Andy) Artist

Anita has little interest in possessions and money. She wants to find self-fulfillment by creating art. But if her art doesn't sell, well, most great artists weren't recognized during their lifetimes. And that's what has happened to her. So she creates for posterity or a small group of admirers that has chosen her to be the inspired bellwether of their conspiratorial community of "true intellectuals" in a tasteless society.

Healing affirmation: I use my abilities to please and enrich all human beings.

7) Nancy (Norm) Naïve

Nancy is so touchingly naive. If someone with a doctorate or some other impressive qualifications tells her that the earth is a disk and the sun only rises and sets because a good-natured UFO commander pushes it with his 10,000-kilometer-long spaceship, she believes it and her eyes open wide in astonishment. She always falls for the salespeople who sell her terribly overpriced nonsense with much fuss, lets herself be hooked by sects that promise her divine well-being but actually just want to exploit her, and believes every book that impressively tells of wonders, immortality, angels, saints, and other splendid things. She likes to go to the channeler or fortune-teller since someone will finally tell her what she should do and not do. And she always looks for Big Daddy to assume responsibility for her life since this step frightens her and she finds it much too complicated. It's too bad that she doesn't want to learn to find her own strength and responsibly go her own way. So she gets taken in by swindlers over and over again. Perhaps she will someday realize that people who relieve her of making decisions and thinking simultaneously also snatch away her opportunity for self-fulfillment and a sense of security within herself.

Healing affirmation: I alone am the only one who can find and walk my path, and I have all the abilities to do it.

8) Steve (Sonja) Specialist

He simply knows everything about his field! And he endeavors to have things also stay this way, which is why he zealously continues to educate himself. Since there basically isn't anything except his specialty that would truly interest him, his circle of friends is limited to people who share his interests. He normally doesn't notice the blinders that he has created for himself by concentrating on his thoughts and actions. However, he sometimes wakes up for a short time, namely, when reality catches up to him and confronts him with demands that he often didn't even know existed, let alone how to deal with them. If he has somehow escaped these dangers, he heaves a sigh of relief and firmly closes his blinders to ban the strange, unfamiliar areas of the world from his sight and finally gets completely involved in his own field again. It's unfortunate that Steve doesn't let the many other wonders of the world into his life. If he were able to, he would possibly discover that instead of missing out on something, he would be gaining an unbelievable amount of quality of life, security, and fulfillment. The abundance of life is only revealed to him when he opens up to its many different areas.

Healing affirmation: I participate in the variety of the world with joy and curiosity.

9) Irene (Isaac) Idealist

Actually, no one should be permitted to drive a car since this pollutes the environment and diminishes our mineral resources. And we should get rid of money. Instead, people should take what they need and give what they have to spare. We should always help others and be there for them. We should simply get rid of the political system, the public officials, and the police, and govern ourselves. Irene talks about the conditions in our world in this way or something similar. She really means well and likes to get together with others who think and feel the same way. Together they talk about how the world should actually be. Sometimes they also attempt to turn their concepts into reality. Yet, the project usually doesn't get beyond the experimental stages, even if these may last for years. Depressed about this development, Irene leaves. However, she soon finds a new ideal for which she can fight. And once again, great ideas and plans are created. Too bad that so much constructive energy is used to build castles in the air. If Irene would use her idealism to bring good things that are possible into the world, many people would be helped and she would finally have the experience of success.

Healing affirmation: I see and use the opportunities for change in the here and now in order to make the future better.

10) Sarah (Swen) Swindler

As long as she can just con someone, she's satisfied. She will naturally always find a good reason for her actions. If she takes something from the department store, it's actually fair to her because the prices are much too high and she's just creating a compensation for them. If she manages to sell an old car for much too much money to someone who doesn't notice that Sarah has had someone use a drill to change the overall mileage on the odometer in her favor, she's happy as a lark. After all, it's the buyer's fault for being so naive. And anyway, the car was still in very good shape. Sarah is more than mistrustful of others. If she notices that someone else actually is very decent, she makes fun of his presumed naiveté and unrealistic approach to life. She believes she can be on the winning side through her behavior and thereby create the security and sense of safeness that she so urgently needs in order to keep suppressing her existential dread. Deep down inside herself, she has intense guilt feelings because of her behavior. She expresses them in her contempt and derogation of honest people. She would also like to be this way, but in order to risk it, she would have to learn to trust as well. And she's afraid to do this, since she would then be at other people's mercy.

Healing affirmation: I always receive what I really need when I trustingly open myself to the devotion of the universe.

Recommended Reading

In this little bibliography, you will find further titles that expand upon the topics mentioned in this book or provide supplementary information and that have been released by Lotus Press.

Reiki—Way of the Heart by Walter Lübeck, Lotus Light/Shangri-La. Introduction to the traditional USUI System of Reiki and comprehensive portrayal of the possibilities for developing the personality with Reiki.

The Complete Reiki Handbook by Walter Lübeck. Lotus Light/Shangri-La. Practical applications of Reiki with many exercises, meditations, and an extensive reference section. A handbook for Reiki therapists and an understandable work foundation for beginners.

The Chakra Handbook by B. Baginsky and S. Sharamon. Lotus Light/Shangri-La. An excellent work for getting involved with the chakra theory in a very practical manner. There is also a Chakra Meditation CD by the authors (with an accompanying brochure), available from Inner Worlds Music.

Aura Healing Handbook by Walter Lübeck. Lotus Press/Shangri-La. Instructions for developing the subtle senses, including reading and interpreting in color the various fields of the aura, the main and secondary chakras, and the meridians, etc. Also contains a profound and extensive depiction of the human energy body.

Pendulum Healing Handbook by Walter Lübeck. Lotus Light/Shangri-La. An introduction to the art of using the pendulum and radiesthesia, which also contains some new information for professionals.

The I Ching or **Book of Changes** by C. F. Boynes, R. Wilhelm (Translator), Vay F. Baynes (Translator), Princeton Univ. Press. One of the most competent and complete books of I Ching. It's worth reading.

The Art of Strategy—A New Translation of Sun Tzu's Classic. The Act of War by Sun Tzu/R. L. Wing, Doubleday. You can use this very old book about war strategy to solve daily problems harmoniously.

Walter Lübeck

Aura Healing Handbook

Learn to Read and Interpret the Aura · Perceive Energy Fields in Color and Utilize Them for Holistic Healing

Anyone can basically learn to see auras. Walter Lübeck's Aura Healing Handbook is a step-by-step instruction manual: By increasing your sensitivity for subtle vibrations, it will ultimately lead you into the fascinating world of seeing auras.

The author explains how to develop your "psychic" powers. He describes the different ways in which you can use these powers and the areas to which you can appl y them. As a result, you can see subtle energies and they will reveal their secrets to you.

Aura reading serves as a diagnostic aid in recognizing health disorders long before they manifest themselves within the body in the form of pain or unwellness. Reading the aura is the first step to healing your energies and emotions in the subtle realm.

224 pages · $15.95
ISBN 0-914955-61-6

Walter Lübeck

Pendulum Healing Handbook

Complete Guidebook on How to Use the Pendulum to Choose Appropriate Remedies for Healing Body, Mind and Spirit.

If you want to learn every aspect of how to use a pendulum, particularly in relation to methods of alternative healing, this book is for you.

This book contains many of the most important pendulum tables from the areas of nutrition, aromas, Bach Flowers, gemstones, chakras, herbs, relationships, etc., and shows how to use them, along with the limits of their application. Walter Lübeck begins with the selection of the right pendulum, shows the correct way to hold it, and also explains the possibilities of energetic cleansing. With 125 pendulum tables.

208 pages · $15.95
ISBN 0-914955-54-3

Dr. Mikao Usui and Frank A. Petter

The Original Reiki Handbook of Dr. Mikao Usui

The Traditional Usui Reiki Ryoho Treatment Positions and Numerous Reiki Techniques for Health and Well-Being

For the first time available outside of Japan: This book will show you the original hand positions from Dr. Usui's handbook. It has been illustrated with 100 colored photos to make it easier to understand. The hand positions for a great variety of health complaints have been listed in detail, making it a valuable reference work for anyone who practices Reiki. Now, that the original handbook has been translated into English, Dr. Usui's hand positions and healing techniques can be studied directly for the first time. Whether you are an initiate or a master, if you practice Reiki you can expand your knowledge dramatically as you follow in the footsteps of a great healer.

80 pages · 100 photos · $14.95
ISBN 0-914955-57-8

Andreas Jell

Healthy with Tachyon

A Complete Handbook Including Basic Principles and Application of Products for Health and Wellness

The comprehensive handbook for using tachyonized materials. A completely new chapter of human history has begun with the possibility of directly applying tachyon energy for healing and development.

Today, you can directly strengthen your powers of self-healing by using tachyonized materials. These powers will then organize perfect healing and development (anti-entropy) through their own dynamic.

Andreas Jell presents the details of all the currently available tachyonized products, as well as how they can be best applied. A brief introduction to the theoretic basis, reports on experiences by users, background knowledge from the fields of medicine and biology, and topics related to the use of tachyon energy provide a comprehensive look at this new, fascinating spiritual/scientific technology.

144 pages · $12.95
ISBN 0-914955-58-6

Herbs and other natural health products and information are often available at natural food stores or metaphysical bookstores. If you cannot find what you need locally, you can contact one of the following sources of supply.

Sources of Supply:

The following companies have an extensive selection of useful products and a long track-record of fulfillment. They have natural body care, aromatherapy, flower essences, crystals and tumbled stones, homeopathy, herbal products, vitamins and supplements, videos, books, audio tapes, candles, incense and bulk herbs, teas, massage tools and products and numerous alternative health items across a wide range of categories.

WHOLESALE:

Wholesale suppliers sell to stores and practitioners, not to individual consumers buying for their own personal use. Individual consumers should contact the RETAIL supplier listed below. Wholesale accounts should contact with business name, resale number or practitioner license in order to obtain a wholesale catalog and set up an account.

Lotus Light Enterprises, Inc.

P. O. Box 1008
Silver Lake, WI 531 70 USA
262 889 8501 (phone)
262 889 8591 (fax)
800 548 3824 (toll free order line)

RETAIL:

Retail suppliers provide products by mail order direct to consumers for their personal use. Stores or practitioners should contact the wholesale supplier listed above.

Internatural

33719 116th Street
Twin Lakes, WI 53181 USA
800 643 4221 (toll free order line)
262 889 8581 office phone
WEB SITE: www.internatural.com

Web site includes an extensive annotated catalog of more than 7000 products that can be ordered "on line" for your convenience 24 hours a day, 7 days a week.